Texts and Monographs in
Economics and Mathematical Systems

Edited by
Martin J. Beckmann and Wilhelm Krelle

Martin J. Beckmann

Tinbergen Lectures on Organization Theory

With a Preface by Jan Tinbergen

Second, Revised and Enlarged Edition

With 19 Figures

Springer-Verlag
Berlin Heidelberg New York
London Paris Tokyo

Prof. Dr. Martin J. Beckmann
Brown University, Providence, RI 02912, USA
and
Institut für Angewandte Mathematik, Technische Universität München
Barerstraße 23, D–8000 München 2, FRG

ISBN 3-540-18515-1 Springer-Verlag Berlin Heidelberg New York
ISBN 0-387-18515-1 Springer-Verlag New York Heidelberg Berlin

The use of registered names, trademarks, etc. in the publication does not imply, even in the absence of a specific statement, that such names are exempt from the relevant protective laws and regulations and therefore free for general use.

Offsetprinting: Weihert-Druck GmbH, Darmstadt. Binding: J. Schäffer GmbH & Co. KG, Grünstadt
2142/3140 – 543210

Preface to the Second Edition

In revising the Tinbergen Lectures I have expanded and restructured the material in an attempt to make the book more readable and more interesting. I have also tried to show more clearly its relevance to managerial and organizational practice.

Some mathematical derivations have been moved to appendices. Certain sections that may be skipped in a first reading have been starred.

Points that should be of interest to management include

- the nature and necessity of rank (4.1, 4.2, 4.4)
- rank assignment by counting up or down (4.3)
- defining an organization's task (6.2)
- calculating the required size of an organization (6.3)
- allocating supervisors in the short run (6.7)
- when uniform spans of control are desirable (6.8)
- how to estimate an organization's implicit span of control (7)
- determining the minimal ranks in supervision (8.3)
- the advantage of flexible department lines (8.4)
- measuring the leanness of an organization (8.5)
- the relationship between average wage and unit labor cost (10.2)
- job allocation in the short run (10.4)
- calculating the cost of supervision for particular jobs (10.5)
- recognizing economic choices in substituting managers for operatives or vice versa (11)
- determining the optimal size of a research team (12)

- setting targets (13.1)
- budgeting under full information (13.2)
- budgeting under imperfect information (13.3)
- sources of information loss (14.1)
- causes and cures for loss of control (14.2 and 19.4)
- staffing decisions in the short, medium and long run
    (16.3, 16.4, 16.6)
- why organizations take over functions of individuals
    (17)
- why and how to reward top management (18)
- team management versus management by delegation (19.1)
- the economic advantage of hierarchy (19)
- the survival of alternatives to hierarchy (20)

In addition, there may be topics of some interest to economic theorists:

- the sources of inequality in organizations (2)
- efficiency in organizational design (8)
- returns to scale in management (10.6, 10.7, 16.7)
- the uses of production functions in organizational
    analysis (15, 16)
- determinants of the wage structure in organizations
    (19.3)

Martin J. Beckmann

Providence, Rhode Island

November, 1987

Preface to the First Edition

In this book Professor Beckmann, with considerable ingenuity, offers a mathematical analysis of productive organizations in the widest sense. Starting with descriptive features he builds up, step by step, production functions, profiting from the rigor of a set of axioms or assumptions and their logical implications. Among the organizations studied hierarchies play a predominant role and are compared with such forms of cooperation as partnerships and "ladders". A number of well-known basic concepts such as span of control, rank, line vs. staff and others serve as starting points. His analysis leads to such refinements as balanced, regular or degenerated organization patterns and interesting comparisons of the efficiency of various structures.

Empirical verification of the axioms or assumptions is not the objective chosen by the author--except a few concrete illustrations--but the book constitutes an excellent basis for such research.

Several of the results obtained take simpler forms for very large hierarchies. The renewed interest, shown in political discussions, in the bureaucratization of both large enterprises and government machinery makes Dr. Beckmann's work highly topical. Discussions (by Bahro) of the GDR and by many other authors of Japanese management as compared with American or Western European are cases in point. Some additional variables may then have to be added, of a psychological nature: for instance satisfaction from work or irritation evoked by excessive supervision.

Having participated in some recent empirical work about the production functions for large entities and about managerial incomes I found Professor Beckmann's coherent and imaginative theoretical setup very helpful. I am certain my evaluation will be shared by those active in related areas of economic research.

Jan Tinbergen
Emeritus Professor
of Development Programming
Erasmus University, Rotterdam

Acknowledgements

While holding the Tinbergen chair at Erasmus Universiteit
Rotterdam in April, May and June of 1982, I gave two courses of
lectures: one on selected problems in spatial economics, and the
present one on the economics of organizations.

Encouraged by my good friend Jean Paelinck I organized the
material of this as a monograph. This task was made simple by the
fact that I had the material for the various chapters available in
a preliminary form as papers written under NSF Grant 79-19376. In
a few places I have drawn on my "Rank in Organizations" to fill in
gaps.

In fact, this is a revision of the material in Chapters I, II,
III, VIII, IX, and X of my earlier book, <u>Rank in Organizations</u>. It
addresses the structural aspects of organizations as distinct from
those concerned with the movement of personnel. The latter will be
reconsidered in a separate monograph.

It is my pleasure to thank Erasmus Universiteit for the honor
of appointing me to the Tinbergen chair in April, May and June of
1982, and the Technical University of Munich for permission to
accept the appointment. I also wish to thank my faithful audience
for their encouragement, interest and stimulating discussion, in
particular Professor Jean Paelinck, Dr. Jean-Pierre Ancot, Dr.
Thijs ten Raa, Dr. Hans Kuiper, Dr. Henk Haverstein, and Dr. Paul
Beije.

I have also benefitted from teaching this subject in
Economics 165 "Economics of Organizations" at Brown University
since 1980.

From 1979 to 1981 I enjoyed the support of the National Science Foundation under grant SES 79-19376 for research on <u>Allocation in Organizations.</u> Some results of this research are found in Chapters 7, 8, 11, 17 and 19.

Grateful acknowledgement is made for comments received (and utilized) from the following individuals:

Professor Carlos Daganzos, University of California, Berkeley.

Dr. David Rosenblatt, Washington, D.C.

Professor Wolfgang Schuler, University of Bielefeld.

It is a pleasure to thank Mrs. Marion Wathey for her beautiful typing of a very messy manuscript, and Dr. J. Fischer, Deutsches Museum and Mrs. Inge Strohlein, Technical University Munich, for making the drawings, and Dr. Mittermeier and Mr. Schaffler for reading an earlier draft of this manuscript and Miss H. Frommelt for her great care in preparing the index.

Martin J. Beckmann

Providence, Rhode Island

November, 1987

Table of Contents

Preface to the Second Edition   v

Preface by Jan Tinbergen   vii

Acknowledgements   ix

Notation   xvii

1. Introduction   1

    1.1 Organizations Defined   1

    1.2 Why Economics of Organization?   1

    1.3 Plan of This Book   4

    1.4 Organizations and Their Environment   6

I. RANK

2. Supervision   8

    2.1 Content of Supervision   9

    2.2 Structure of Supervision   10

    2.3 A Directed Graph   11

    2.4 Alternative Description   12

    2.5 Organization Charts in Practice   14

3. Control   16

    3.1 Structure   16

    3.2 Control Sets   17

    3.3 Partial Order   17

   *3.4 Further Remarks   19

4. Rank   21

    4.1 Motivation   21

    4.2 Simple Ordering   22

    4.3 Counting Supervisory Relationships   24

    4.4 Meaning of Rank   29

    4.5 Rank and Precedence   30

    Problems   31

5. Distance   33

    5.1 Organization Charts as Graphs   33

    5.2 Communication Networks   33

    5.3 Locating the President   37

   *5.4 Enumeration   40

                    II.   PERFECT MANAGEMENT

6. Numbers of Positions   41

    6.1 Span of Control   41

    6.2 Quantification of Task   43

    6.3 Constant Span of Control   44

    6.4 Disaggregation of Task   48

    6.5 Full-Time Assignments   51

    6.6 Supervisory Load and Effort   55

    6.7 Allocation of Managers in the Short Run   56

    6.8 Average Span of Control and Output   57

    6.9 Spans of Control Decreasing with Rank   59

7. Estimation   63

    7.1 From M and Q   63

    7.2 From Lists of Positions by Rank   64

    7.3 Other Estimates   67

8. Assignment   71

    8.1 The Problem of Implementation   71

    8.2 Integer Assignments   72

    8.3 Minimizing Ranks   73

    8.4 Flexible or Rigid Department Lines   77

    8.5 Leanness of Organizations   78

   *8.6 Support Structure   81

         Problems   83

9.	Regular Organization	85
	9.1 Construction	85
	9.2 Properties	86
	9.3 Average Rank	87
	*9.4 Average Distance	88
10.	Costs	90
	10.1 Salary Schedules	90
	10.2 Average Wage and Unit Labor Cost	92
	10.3 Cost Minimizing Organizational Designs	94
	10.4 Job Allocation in the Short Run	96
	10.5 Minimizing Unit Labor Costs	98
	10.6 Cost and Scale for Regular Organizations	101
	10.7 Cost and Scale for Nonregular Organizations	104

III. PRODUCTIVITY AND STRUCTURE

11.	Substitution of Management and Operative Inputs: Welfare Agency	109
	11.1 A Queuing Model	109
	11.2 Analysis	112
	11.3 Discussion	115
	11.4 Generalization	116
12.	Information Costs: Research Teams	122
	12.1 Model	124
	12.2 Production Function	126
	12.3 Checking	128
13.	Loss of Information in Simple Organizations	130
	13.1 Setting Targets	130
	13.2 Budgeting with Full Information	134
	13.3 Incomplete Information	139
14.	Loss of Information and Control in Multi-Level Organizations	143
	14.1 Loss of Information	143
	14.2 Loss of Control	145

15. Uses of Production Functions: Simple Organizations 148

    15.1 Attainable Output 148

    15.2 Labor Requirements 149

    15.3 Supervisory Input 150

    15.4 Minimizing the Cost of Given Output 151

    15.5 Increasing Returns to Scale 153

16. Uses of Production Functions: Multi-Level

    Organizations 155

    16.1 A Production Function for Management 155

    16.2 Allocation of Inputs 159

    16.3 Short Run 160

    16.4 Medium Run: Optimal Spans of Control 163

    16.5 Medium Run: Cost Functions 165

    16.6 Long Run: Optimal Number of Ranks 166

    16.7 Long Run: Cost Functions 167

IV. ADVANTAGE AND MOTIVATION

17. Organizations vs. Individuals 170

    17.1 Organization of Individual Effort 171

    17.2 Larger Output: Simple Organization 173

    17.3 Advantage of Simple Organization 177

    17.4 Utilizing Better Qualified Personnel 180

18. Management Motivation: Principal and Agent 182

    18.1 Introduction 182

    18.2 Managers as Principals 183

    18.3 Linear Homogeneous Production Function 186

    18.4 Managers as Agents 189

    18.5 Increasing Returns to Scale 192

19. The Economics of Hierarchy 196

    19.1 Management by Delegation 196

    19.2 Optimization 198

    19.3 Discussion: Emerging Wage Structure 200

    19.4 Loss of Control 201

19.5 Team Work at the Top   204
19.6 Long Run   205
19.7 Organizational Modes of an Industry   209

20. Alternatives to Hierarchy: Partnerships   211
20.1 Partnership Defined   211
20.2 Equal Sharing and Full Time Work   212
20.3 Advantage of Partnership: Fixed Shares   216
20.4 Proportional Rewards   221

CONCLUSION

Appendix A. Deriving Supervisory Relationships
    from Control   227
Appendix B. Average Span of Control and More Graph Theory 228
Appendix C.   Proof of Lemma for Section 6.9   230

Selected Bibliography   232
Name Index   241
Subject Index   242

Notation

(Symbols used in more than one chapter)

α	output elasticity of labor
a	salary factor
b	productivity coefficient
β	output elasticity of supervision
C	total (wage) cost
$\bar{c}$	unit cost
$F(\cdot,\cdot)$	production function
$f(\cdot,\cdot)$	linear homogeneous production function
$\phi(x)$	single factor production function
ρ	factor of control loss
g	organization's surplus
h	surplus under management by delegation
k	moving cost
n_r	number of positions of rank r (integer)
N_r	number of positions of rank r or higher
N	total number of positions in the organization
π	product price
q	measure of ability
Q	size of the task, number of operatives required
r	rank
R	presidential rank, also scale of the organization
w_r	wage in rank r
$w_R^{\star}$	presidential wage
W	wage bill
$\bar{w}$	average wage
x_r	positions in rank r (continuum)
y	output
y_r	output of managers, "management" in efficiency units
z_r	staff positions in rank r
$\|$	end of proof

1 Introduction

<u>1.1   Organizations Defined</u>

"Observation shows us that all associations are instituted
for the purpose of attaining some good" (Aristotle, Politics,
Book 1, Chapter 1). For purpose of this monograph organizations
are defined as associations of persons
- set up for a well-defined purpose
- requiring more than one person's effort
- utilizing resources
- not using exchange in markets but other methods
  of coordination.

A family or nation is not an organization (their ends being
too broad) nor is an industry unless it is an organized monopoly,
(the market being used for coordination) nor is a one-person
firm. But organizations as here defined include business firms
as well as nonprofit organizations, government and its various
branches, the military, churches and last not least universities
and research organizations.

<u>1.2   Why Economics of Organization?</u>

All things are legitimate objects for economic inquiry;
organizations playing a prominent part in modern life are
particularly worthy subjects of economic analysis. They are too
important to be left to the sociologists.

In economic theory organizations appear as "economic agents"
in their roles as
- suppliers of goods and services
- demanders of labor and other resources.

They thus participate in markets as buyers and sellers just as
ordinary persons do. These agents may be treated as black boxes
whose inside is unknown and whose outward behavior shows certain

regularities. But can we assume that organizations behave exactly like persons? Here is a first question for economic analysis. Under what conditions do organizations act as utility or profit maximizers? To answer this we must peer into the black box.

For a broader view of the economics of organizations consider the five basic functions that, Frank Knight tells us, every economic system must perform.

1.   It must determine the ends--it must decide what goods and services should be produced in what quantities. Generally an organization must define its objectives, its task, and quantify these.

2.   "Resources must be allocated" among the various branches and ultimately the individual members of an organization. In fact the members themselves may have to be recruited, trained, assigned and moved among the various functions to be performed in the organization.

3.   "Within short periods of time it is necessary to adjust the use of relatively fixed supplies ... of goods and services" (Stigler, p. 32). This can mean making the best use of an insufficient number of personnel or conversely the decision of who should be let go to save the organization in periods of financial distress.

4.   "The product must be distributed among the members" of the organization. This means the setting of compensation in its various forms.

5.   "Provision must be made for the maintenance and expansion of the organization" (Stigler, p. 32).

Three basic questions emerge in the study of these economic functions of organizations.

A. Since organizations are by definition multi-personal, to what extent can they institute and obtain benefits from a <u>division of labor</u>?

B. How can <u>efficiency</u> in the allocation of resources be defined and achieved?

C. What determines the degree of <u>inequality</u> in the distribution of effort and rewards in organizations?

The specific flavor of the economics of organizations derives from the fact that organizations do not (normally) use markets for the internal allocation of resources but rely on "<u>command and control</u>"--the fundamental alternative to voluntary exchange. Concretely, the act of joining our organization may be voluntary. But the contract will specify that as a condition of membership one must obey orders by "authorized persons". Why are people willing to give up part of their freedom and submit to authority?

In a market economy, based on voluntary decisions of individuals, the answer can only be that most individuals prefer working for organizations to being independent. In part this may be because certain activities can no longer be performed on competitive terms by independent individuals. If you want to do research, you must join a research organization or university. Even poets may have to become teachers employed by organizations.

Command and control refers to the allocation of personnel. In the use of other resources and in the recruiting of personnel markets are still utilized. The interaction of these two modes of allocation requires suitable <u>institutional arrangements</u>. Economic analysis can focus attention on these (Simon, Putterman, Williamson) or it can look at the <u>interaction of decisions</u>. A multi-personal organization can function only if the actions of the members are coordinated. Command and control requires that information be passed between the various decision makers, and between the decision makers and the operatives performing the tasks of the organization. For command to be effective, _motivation_ is needed. Where control is perfect, avoidance of punishments such as reprimand or dismissal may be enough to ensure adequate performance. Where control is imperfect, positive inducements may be appropriate substitutes. The question is, how can organization members be best induced to perform the functions required for the discharge of the organization's tasks?

1.3 Plan of This Book

These are difficult questions and economic theory does not have all the answers yet. Research is underway at various frontiers. In this book we will consider the following topics, among others.

I. Rank

What are the sources of inequality in organizations? Why are ranks needed? We show these to be a byproduct of supervision. Supervision is required to assure and coordinate the discharge of the subtask into which the grand task of an organization is broken down.

II. Perfect Management

Suppose supervision is sufficiently intensive to assure perfectly adequate performance of those who discharge the actual task of the organization, the operatives. Let these tasks be quantified in terms of required numbers of operatives. Under these conditions, what can be said about efficient organizational structures? How can the costs to the organization be calculated for the various tasks performed by operatives? How do costs vary with size, are there economies or diseconomies of scale?

III. Imperfect Communication and Control

How do imperfections in command and control affect the relationship between inputs and outputs of an organization? Can these be captured by production functions? How do institutional arrangements translate into properties of these production functions?

IV. Advantage and Motivation

What are the motives for starting an organization, the economic costs and rewards? When are partnerships, which share rewards and (sometimes) rotate management, preferred to proprietary organizations in which the boss appropriates the surplus (if any)?

Numerous smaller questions will be encountered along the way: the optimal span of control, the modelling of managerial functions, the reasons for various salary structures, the different possibilities for assigning rank, etc.

Other Approaches

Organizations being the important institutions they are in modern life, have attracted analysts from various fields. Lines of approach include
- legal: studies the scopes and limits of organizational activities
- sociological: studies the structure and function of organizations as interacting systems of persons, both at the formal and informal levels
- managerial: studies how organizations can and should be managed i.e., "made to work"
- OR (operations research): gives aid to decision makers by proposing efficient solutions to partial management problems.

These various approaches--and particularly the second and third--have generated a vast literature of uneven quality.

Whether economic theory can contribute something on its own, remains to be shown.

1.4 Organizations and Their Environment

In this monograph the focus is on the internal problems of organizations. But their external relationships must be recognized at least in passing. These relationships arise out of the following fundamental problems:

1. Direction Who sets the goals of the organization? In some cases these are determined internally by the organizer as owner and chief executive of the organization. More common is that direction and goals are the responsibility of an outside board of governors or trustees.

2. Clients: Who benefits from the organization? In some cases clientele is identical with membership as in a club. But more often the clients are outside customers, or recipients of grants, etc.

3. Sources: Who supplies resources to the organization? Every organization needs outside sources of funds, of personnel and/or goods and services. A business firm obtains its income from sales to customers, a government agency may obtain both fees from beneficiaries and funds out of specific or general taxes.

Personnel may be recruited from specific sources, e.g., the holders of college degrees, or diplomas of specified quality, or persons with specialized knowledge or experience. We assume that personnel as well as other inputs are traded in well-established markets.

4. <u>Constraints</u>: Who limits the activities of an organization?

In the first place the law, which may prohibit some and restrict other actions. Regulating agencies may impose constraints in a specific area of activity. Finally, and often most importantly competing organizations impose constraints through the market.

More generally, the economic system within which an organization exists, imposes the most severe limits on its operations. It depends on the system whether an organization can freely purchase and sell goods and services or is dependent on allocations by central planners.

In this book we consider organizations only within the framework of a market economy. Unless said otherwise, we assume that the markets in which an organization participates, are all perfectly competitive.

I Rank

2 Supervision

Organizations are charged with tasks that exceed the capacity
of a single individual. To handle large tasks, one must divide and
further subdivide them in such a way that the final units obtained
by this sequence of subdivision can be worked on independently of
each other. At each stage the subtasks of the next lower stage
must be put together. This could be a physical process of assembly
from sub-assemblies. More often it is a decision making process,
where each stage works out the details of the next higher stage and
delegates further details to the next lower stage. A prerequisite
is that such "factoring" of a task into parts is technically
feasible repeatedly.

In a big orchestra it is not, and the conductor may have to
direct 150 musicians plus untold singers all at once. In tax
collection, a nice division can be made by regions and districts,
by types of tax, by income classes of taxpayers, etc. A university
can be divided neatly into schools, colleges and departments
although the interdisciplinary interaction tends to suffer from
this. (As a corrective "centers" and "programs" and committees are
created to cut across departmental lines.) For better or worse,
all large organizations must divide, subdivide and subdivide again
into workable units.

To get the task done, the individual contributions must be
coordinated. In the absence of markets this is done through an
assignment of accountability for results. But in order to get the
results, to get the job done, persons who are accountable must also
have authority. Thus whoever performs part of a job is made to

report to the person who is in charge and held accountable for the performance of this job. We call this relationship <u>supervision</u> and interpret it broadly.

Thus the supervisor too must report to a supervisor, and so on. The only exception to this rule is to the top person in the organization who although accountable for the performance of the entire organization, reports to no one: the president. An organization with supervision is called a <u>hierarchical organization</u>.

These notions are formalized in the following abstract description of supervision in a hierarchical organization. These formal properties apply in all hierarchical organizations even though the content of supervision may vary considerably among organizations from collaboration with a senior author (in a research organization) to the absolute power of command in a military organization.

2.1 <u>Content of Supervision</u>

Supervision can mean many different things in different organizations, but often includes the following:

> hiring
> induction
> training
> monitoring
> checking
> collaborating
> correcting
> evaluating
> criticizing
> rewarding
> administering
> proposing for promotion
> firing

Also the minuteness and closeness of supervision varies greatly among organizations.

The similarity between hierarchical organizations is due to the fact that regardless of its content the structure of supervision obeys the same principles in all organizations.

2.2 Structure of Supervision

Formally, a <u>hierarchical organization</u> is a labelled set of elements (positions, organization members) and a binary relationship supervision defined by a function $sp(\ )$ on the set of elements. This function $sp(\ )$ and the relationship it defines must satisfy certain requirements.

Postulate Set I

Postulate 1: There exists a unique element p .

Postulate 2: For every $i \neq p$ there exists a unique j such that

$$(1) \qquad j = sp(i) \qquad\qquad i \neq p.$$

Postulate 3: The relationship sp is
1)   irreflexive: not $i = sp(i)$;
2)   asymmetric: if $j = sp(i)$ then not $i = sp(j)$;
3)   acyclic: if $j_1 = sp(i)$

$$j_2 = sp(j_1)$$
$$\vdots \qquad \vdots$$
$$j_n = sp(j_{n-1})$$

$$\text{then not} \qquad i = sp(j_n).$$

Postulate 1 states that the president is not supervised by anyone in the organization. Postulate 2 states the principle of "unified command". Every person, except the president, reports to one and only one supervisor.

Postulate 3 rules out self-supervision, mutual-supervision, and cliques as contrary to the requirements of "effective supervision" in practice. A pertinent example is mentioned by Adam Smith (<u>Wealth of Nations</u>, Everyman edition, London, 1931, p. 247):

> "If the authority to which he is subject resides in the
> body corporate, the college, or university, of which he
> himself is a member, and in which the greater part of the
> other members are, like himself, persons who either are
> or ought to be teachers, they are likely to make a common
> cause, to be all very indulgent to one another, and every
> man to consent that his neighbor may neglect his duty,
> provided he himself is allowed to neglect his own. In
> the university of Oxford, the greater part of the public
> professors have, for these many years, given up
> altogether even the pretence of teaching."

2.3 A Directed Graph

The supervisory relationship may be represented in terms of a <u>directed graph</u> (digraph) such that a directed arc connects j to i whenever

$$j = sp(i).$$

Postulate Set 1 is then succinctly summarized as

<u>Lemma</u>: The directed graph of supervisory relationships is a
    tree with p as its root.
Recall that the root (or source) of a directed tree is the unique point from which a directed path exists to every other point of the tree (Harary, 1971).

This (directed) graph is usually called the <u>organizational chart</u>.

Examples of (simple) organizational charts are given in Figures 4.1 (p. 22), 4.2 (p. 27), 5.1 (p. 35), 6.1 (p. 47), 6.2 (p. 53), 9.1 (p. 90), 10.1 (p. 104). A number of properties of this digraph are discussed and proved in Beckmann (1983). For purposes of organization theory, the following are the most interesting.

. For every position i the organizational chart contains a
unique directed path from p to i. This path describes the
"chain of command" that links the president to every organization
member. Uniqueness means that there is exactly one "channel" to be
used in communicating with supervisors and eventually the
president.

. Consider the subset of positions in the organization chart
whose chains of command pass through a given element j. This
subset is also a hierarchical organization (as defined on
page 9) with j as its president.

Thus those parts of an organization that are headed by one
person may be studied as organizations in their own right.

. Three types of nodes may be distinguished which represent
three types of position in the organization:

1) a single source (or root): the president;
2) at least one sink (or endpoint): non-supervisory
   positions, operatives;
3) nodes having one inbound and at least one outbound arc
   (transit points): supervisory positions other than the
   president.

2.4 Alternative Description

An alternative specification of the supervisory relationship
in terms of its digraph is as follows:

Postulate Set II:

Postulate 1a:

For every node i there exists at most one predecessor node
j, i.e., a j such that

$$j = sp(i);$$

Postulate 2a:

The organization chart is (weakly) connected;

Postulate 3a:

The organization chart contains no cycles.

Weakly connected means that every pair of nodes is connected through a semi-path. A semi-path is a chain of directed arcs whose directions need not be the same.

In this characterization there is no need to introduce the distinguishing position p from the beginning. It is the result of connectivity and acyclicity.

Theorem 1:   There exists one and only one source, i.e., an element p with no supervisor

$$i \mid p \to p.$$

Proof: Start with any element j and consider its supervisor i_1 = sp(j), the supervisor of i_1, i_2 = sp(i_1), etc. This sequence must end, at the latest when all elements of the finite organization graph have been listed. For acyclicity rules out that any element may appear twice. Therefore, there is at least one source p.

Suppose there are two, p_1 and p_2. By weak connectedness a semipath exists between p_1 and p_2. The direction points away from the endpoints p_1 and p_2. At some intermediate point there must be a reversal of direction. This implies more than one supervisor for the element at which directions are reversed. ||

This postulate set exploits the weak connectedness of the organization to relax the necessity of supervision. The distinguished element p need not be postulated here but can be proved to exist.

2.5 Organization Charts in Practice

For supervision to function each organization member need know only

   i)   who is his/her immediate supervisor

   ii) who are his/her immediate subordinates?

In organizations charged with intelligence, this is sometimes all a member knows about the structure of the organization.

In large organizations, even without any attempt at secrecy, an organization member typically knows only:

   i)   all persons on the chain of command from the president to the organization member

   ii) those placed under the same immediate supervisor as the organization member (the colleagues in the department)

   iii) one's immediate subordinates.

By contrast, the <u>organizational chart</u> is a complete description of the structure of an organization. The organization chart can be constructed entirely from a list in which for each person the supervisor is named.

We can also visualize the organizational chart as a network of strings where each knot is a position, and each string a supervisory relationship. The knot representing the presidential position is not identified but must be specified. Such a string model represents a complete map of the organization.

Conventionally the organizational chart is drawn as a graph in which the supervisor is placed above his/her subordinates and connected to them by lines usually drawn in horizontal and vertical directions only (but without arrows).

Ambiguities can arise in actual organizational charts when

   i)   special relationships are distinguished from ordinary "line" supervision: staff relationships (this ambiguity disappears when a staff person is also considered a subordinate, subject to supervision by his/her immediate boss).

  ii) More than one person is assigned as supervisor to a given organization member. (In that case the postulates of supervision must be changed accordingly, see below problem 4.1).

No problem arises when the "assistant department chairman" supervises some of the department members and the chairman supervises the others directly.

Organization charts show more than just supervisory relation-ships. Typically they also present the following information:

  a) The division of the organization into branches and departments,

  b) the official channels of communication,

  c) the career tracks,

  d) the levels or "ranks" of organization members (Chapter 4),

  e) their spans of control (Section 6.1).

3 Control

Supervision is a relationship between a person and his/her immediate boss or between a supervisor and his/her immediate subordinates. Another relationship is that between a boss and all persons placed under the boss's authority by means of direct or indirect supervision exercised if need be through intermediate supervisors. This relationship is called control. Its formal definition is as follows.

3.1 Structure

<u>Definition</u>:

  i controls j, $i \rightarrow j$ if $i = sp(j)$

  or if there exist $j_1, j_2, \ldots, j_m$ such that

$$i = sp(j_1)$$
$$j_1 = sp(j_2)$$
$$\cdot\ \cdot\ \cdot\ \cdot\ \cdot$$
$$j_{m-1} = sp(j_m)$$
$$j_m = sp(j).$$

<u>Theorem 1</u>

The postulates for supervision imply the following properties of control $\rightarrow$. Control is

 i. irreflexive: not $i \rightarrow i$;

 ii. asymmetric: if $i \rightarrow k$, then not $k \rightarrow i$;

 iii. transitive: if $i \rightarrow j$ and $j \rightarrow k$, then $i \rightarrow k$.

<u>Proof</u>: By construction, $\rightarrow$ is transitive. If a chain of supervisors exists from i to k and a chain of supervisors exists from k to j, then this defines a chain of supervisors from i to j.

$\rightarrow$ is irreflexive since sp is irreflexive.
$\rightarrow$ is <u>asymmetric</u>. Suppose that $i \rightarrow j$ and $j \rightarrow i$. Then this defines a closed chain of supervisors from i to i, violating the acyclicity of sp. $\|$

3.2 <u>Control Sets</u>

The concept of control may also be described as a correspondence between an element i and the set of elements controlled by i, the control set S_i. This set is empty when i is not a supervisor.

<u>Definition</u>: Control Set S_i

$$S_i = \{j \mid i \rightarrow j\}.$$

<u>Proposition</u>: $i \rightarrow j$ if and only if $S_i \supset S_j$.

<u>Proposition</u>: The president is the unique organization member whose control set is the entire organization minus himself.

<u>Proposition</u>: The control set of any member plus this member is also an organization, i.e., a set of positions (persons) satisfying postulate set I for a hierarchical organization.

The partial ordering "control" is a simple ordering if for every pair i,k $i \neq k$ either $i \rightarrow k$ or $k \rightarrow i$. This excludes the possibility that both i and k are controlled by a third member j while neither controls the other. Therefore, the organization must be a ladder (Figure 6.1c). Some further properties of control sets are given in Appendix A.

3.3 <u>Partial Order</u>

It is well-known that any relationship with the properties stated in Theorem 1 generates a partial ordering on a set. In fact,

__Theorem 2__: The irreflexive, asymmetric and transitive relationship "control" defines a __strict partial ordering__ of the organization members.

The economic implications of this mathematical fact are far-reaching. Supervision creates inequality, not just between supervisor and immediate subordinate but an ordering or ranking along all chains of control extending all the way from the president to the lowest operative.

Like every partial ordering, the ordering by control may be stated in terms of set inclusion, here the inclusion of control sets. Thus

$$i > j \quad \text{if} \quad S_j \supset S_i$$

where S_i is the set of persons controlled by i, the control set of i.

__Definition__: An organization is a ladder if all organization members can be arranged on a supervisory chain

$$p \to i_1 \to i_2 \to \cdots \to i_{N-1}.$$

Here N is the number of members of the organizations. Ladders are found in pecking orders among chickens or as a "precedence ordering" in an organization (Section 4.5).

__Corollary__. When the organization is not a ladder, then there exists a pair of positions i,j such that

$$\text{neither} \quad i \to j$$

$$\text{nor} \quad j \to i.$$

For example in Figure 4.1, this is true for the pairs 5 and 3 or 1 and 2 or 5 and 6, etc.

3.4 Further Remarks

As far as supervision and control are concerned nothing more than a partial order is implied or needed. Any ordering of organization members by other criteria should, however, be consistent with the partial ordering by control in order to avoid organizational conflict.

<u>Definition</u>: i is a maximal element in a partially ordered subset S if there exists no $j \in S$ such that $j \to i$.

<u>Proposition</u>: Every subset S of the organization contains a maximal element.
(This is a well-known theorem about partially ordered sets, cf. Sen, p. 11.)

<u>Proof</u>: Take any $i \in S$. If there is no predecessor j such that $j_1 \to i$, then i is a maximal element. Otherwise, continue the argument with the predecessor j_1 as the element under consideration. In this way construct a chain $j_m \to j_{m-1} \cdots j_1 \to i$. No element may occur more than once in this chain. The chain must stop at the latest when all elements in S are included. $\|$

The economic interpretation is that any subset of the organization contains at least one ranking member, i.e., member not outranked by any other member.

If the subset is a control set plus the controlling element, then the ranking member (the controlling element) ranks, in fact, above all other members of the subset.

Suppose that not the relationships "supervision" but the relationships "control" are known for an organization. Can one recover the relationship supervision from this, i.e., determine the supervisor k for each person from a knowledge of the control sets? The supervisor of j is in fact found as the intersection of all control sets S_i that contain j.

$$k = sp(j) \quad iff \quad \{k\} = \bigcap_{i:j\varepsilon S_i} S_i$$

4 Rank

4.1 <u>Motivation</u>

Some organizations deliberately avoid any ordering of members beyond that necessitated by control. Others go so far as to establish a complete strict ordering by precedence, but in such a way that precedence is consistent with and supplementary to control.

Most organizations operate between these extremes. They establish a simple ordering which, unlike precedence, is not strict. The equivalence classes in this simple ordering are called ranks.

Rank may be designated by specific titles or by classes of titles. They may be numbered. Our convention will be to designate ranks r by

$$r = 0,1,2, \ldots, R.$$

where R denotes the highest rank, the rank of the president. Gaps in the numbering system will not be allowed.

The reasons for establishing a complete ordering of positions by rank are partly social and partly economic. The most important economic reason is to have a simple, consistent and transparent method for setting salaries and other perquisites of office. The social reasons are to remove any potential conflict about a person's standing within the organization, in general, and with respect to any other organization member in particular.

4.2 Simple Ordering

While the partial ordering of positions was strict, the simple
ordering will be so only in the case of a ladder, when the number
of ranks equals the number of positions. In all other cases there
are fewer ranks than positions so that at least one rank is
occupied by more than one position. This means that the simple
ordering is no longer strict but contains equivalence classes

$$E_i = \{j \mid i \sim j\}.$$

The equivalence relation $\sim$ is reflexive, symmetric and
transitive. Complete ordering means that
for any two organization members i,j either

$$i \rightarrow j \quad \text{or}$$

$$i \sim j \quad \text{or}$$

$$j \rightarrow i.$$

For the last statement we also write $i \leftarrow j$.
Now let rank be designated not only by title but also by numbers.
Rank is a function on equivalence classes. The complete ordering
of organization members is then homomorphic to the ordering of
integers.

$$i \left\{ \begin{matrix} \rightarrow \\ \sim \\ \leftarrow \end{matrix} \right\} j \quad \text{whenever} \quad r(i) \left\{ \begin{matrix} > \\ = \\ < \end{matrix} \right\} r(j).$$

Consider the following rule for generating a complete ordering
among organization members: Two positions i,j are considered
equivalent when neither supervises the other. Is this consistent
with the strict partial order defined by control?

As an example consider the organization

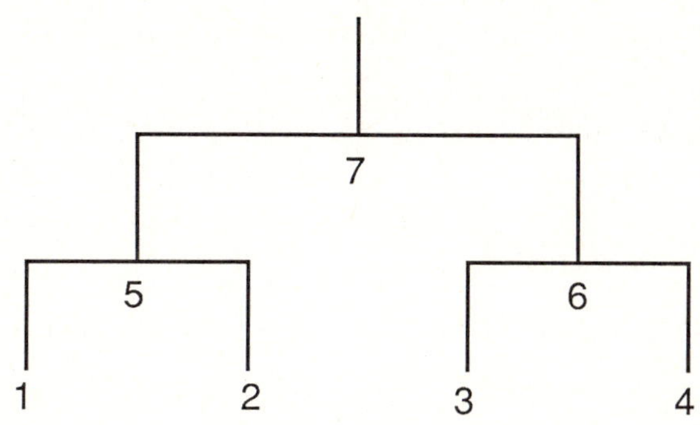

Figure 4.1. Organizational Chart

Now
$$C_7 = \{1,2,3,4,5\}$$
$$C_6 = \{3,4\}$$
$$C_5 = \{1,2\}$$
$$C_4 = \phi$$
$$C_3 = \phi$$
$$C_2 = \phi$$
$$C_1 = \phi.$$

Since 1 does not control $3 \varepsilon C_1$ and 3 does not supervise $5 \varepsilon C_3$ one has

$$1 \frown 3 \frown 5, \quad \text{but} \quad 5 \to 1, \quad \text{a contradiction.}$$

To obtain a ranking that is consistent with the strict partial ordering of control $\to$ one may either count supervisory relationships or compare the sizes of control sets. We consider the second method first. Let $|S_i|$ = number of persons controlled by i and define a complete ordering of organization members by the numerical ordering of $|S_i|$. Thus

$$i \quad \left\{ \begin{array}{c} \rightarrow \\ \frown \\ \leftarrow \end{array} \right\} \quad j \qquad \text{whenever} \qquad |S_i| \left\{ \begin{array}{c} > \\ = \\ < \end{array} \right\} |S_j| .$$

Notice that the simple ordering by size of control sets is consistent with the partial $\rightarrow$ defined by control, for $i \rightarrow k$ means

$$k \in S_i \quad \text{which implies} \quad S_i \supset S_k, \quad \text{hence}$$

$$|S_i| > |S_k| .$$

The converse does not follow.

4.3 Counting Supervisory Relationships

Another natural way of setting up a complete ordering among organization members is by counting supervisory relationships-- either from the top down or from the bottom up or in some intermediate way.

In a regular organization (Section 9) this produces the same rank as by counting the number of persons controlled. In general, the results are different and it is more difficult to count the numbers of persons controlled. Changes in employment can easily upset such a rank structure, while that based on counting supervisory links tend to remain stable. Rank defined by the number of people controlled is, therefore, uncommon.

From now on the complete ordering of the members of an organization will be discussed in terms of its equivalence classes, the ranks. Furthermore, we assume that these ranks are numbered and that the larger number represents the higher rank.

In assigning a rank r to every position in an hierarchical organization the objective of creating comparability among all positions is achieved best by limiting the range of ranks as far as possible. The minimum range equals the longest chain of command (economy of rank numbers). Define distance on a line of command

$$\ell(i,j) = \text{number of links in chain of command from } i$$
$$\text{to } j \text{ or } j \text{ to } i \text{ if it exists}$$
$$= 0 \quad \text{otherwise.}$$

<u>Proposition</u>: $\text{Min} \quad R = \underset{i,j}{\text{Max}} \quad \ell(i,j)$

$$= \underset{j}{\text{Max}} \quad \ell(p,j).$$

For convenience we choose the lowest rank to be zero and the highest rank R to be the smallest integer consistent with the following

<u>Rank Assignment Principle</u>: A supervisor's rank must be strictly larger than a subordinate's rank.

$$r(sp(i)) > r(i). \tag{1}$$

Two simple methods of rank assignment are
<u>Counting down</u>
The president's rank is R

$$\rho(p) = R. \tag{2}$$

A subordinate's rank is one less than the supervisor's rank.

$$\rho(i) = \rho(sp(i)) - 1. \tag{3}$$

From the definition of R it follows that at least one operative (on a longest chain) has rank zero.

Counting up

The rank of any nonsupervisory position is zero.

$$\lambda(i) = 0 \quad \text{when} \quad S_i = \phi \tag{4}$$

where S_i is the control set of i.
The rank of a supervisor is one higher than the highest rank of any one in his control set

$$\lambda(i) = 1 + \underset{j \varepsilon S_i}{\text{Max}} \ \lambda(j). \tag{5}$$

(Note: the same rank λ is obtained when S_i is replaced by the set of all positions directly supervised by i.)

Theorem: Let $r(i)$, $0 \leqslant r(i) \leqslant R$ be any rank assignment satisfying the assignment principle (1). Then

$$\lambda(i) \leqslant r(i) \leqslant \rho(i). \tag{6}$$

Counting up results in the lowest and counting down in the highest ranks consistent with the assignment principle.
The proof is given by means of the following lemmas:

Lemma 1: There is a longest chain of command. On this chain ranks are unique.

Proof: Otherwise R would not be equal to the length of the maximum chain.
A longest chain is also called critical. Any shorter chains is called noncritical.

<u>Lemma 2</u>: For all other ranks R--(number of links to president) is an upper bound of rank r.

<u>Proof</u>: Each supervisory relationship requires at least a unit increase in rank.

<u>Lemma 3</u>: The number of links to the bottom end of a chain is a lower bound on rank.

<u>Proof</u>: The minimum rank at the end of a chain is $r = 0$. From 0 on rank must increase by at least unity for each supervisory link.

<u>Corollary</u>: On each noncritical chain of command the lower bound rank $\lambda(i)$ must jump by more than unity in at least one supervisory relationship.

<u>Proof</u>: A noncritical chain is shorter than R.

<u>Corollary</u>: On every noncritical chain the bottom rank under counting down is positive $\rho > 0$, hence all $\rho > 0$.

<u>Corollary</u>: On any noncritical chain either $r > 0$ for all positions or r jumps by more than unity between a subordinate and the supervisor.

<u>Definition</u>: An organizational structure is called balanced when all chains of command are critical.

<u>Lemma 4</u>: In a balanced structure all ranks are uniquely determined.

<u>Proof</u>: By definition and Lemma 1.
Examples of balanced organizations are given in Figures 4.1, 5.2 and 9.1.

<u>Corollary</u>: In a balanced structure all nonsupervisory personnel has rank zero.

<u>Lemma 5</u>: Under counting up, the number of positions cannot increase with rank:

$$n_{r+1} \leqq n_r.$$

<u>Proof</u>: All nonsupervisory positions have rank $\lambda = 0$. For every position of rank $\lambda > 0$, the number of arrows entering from above is one and the number of arrows exiting is greater or equal to one. Hence,

$$n_{r-1} \geqq n_r, \qquad r > 0,$$

$$n_{r+1} \leqq n_r, \qquad r = 0, \ldots, R-1.$$

All rank concepts used so far were ordinal. Once rank differences are defined, rank becomes cardinal. Successive ranks need not be equi-distant, however. For instance, the step from colonel to general may be considered larger than that from lieutenant colonel to colonel.

Cardinal ranks may be represented by cardinal numbers, usually by integers.

In the following we assume that successive ranks are equi-distant and we represent ranks by the integers

$$r = 0,1, \ldots, R.$$

For cardinal ranks, the concepts of <u>average rank</u> and <u>expected value of ranks</u> may be defined and applied (see below).

4.4 Meaning of Rank

The most important attributes or implications of rank are: power, prestige, and money income.

Power is directly exercised over the organization members in the control set of the rank holder, the set of persons reached through a chain of supervision or command. Supervisory power in a hierarchical organization is in fact restricted by the formalities first spelled out by Max Weber in his definition and analysis of bureaucracy (1925). Power or authority declines sharply outside the organizational division headed by the rank holder, but still exists to some extent "by courtesy".

For rank to be economically meaningful, compensation must increase with rank when all is added up: salary, bonus, stock options and the tax exempt income generated by expense accounts, insurance, use of cars, clubs and recreation facilities and other perquisites of rank. Compensation is not a simple linear function of rank, there is more reason to expect that utility is (Section 10.1). Diminishing marginal utility of income and the progressive income tax imply that income should be a convex function of rank.

The question of the economic determinants of salary schemes is answered differently in the case of organizations that have no interaction with labor markets except at the entry level of rank zero (church, military) and those that operate in competitive labor markets by hiring and firing personnel at all levels.

Prestige, not properly an economic variable, is a residual category that reflects all attributes of rank other than power and money income. The prestige aspect may be expressed by such marks of rank as titles, uniforms, the size, location, furnishings, of office and the number of its windows, parking and the availability and attractiveness of support personnel.

Prestige of rank enhanced possibly by the organization's prestige is carried over to some extent into the outside world. In this way rank in organizations may be transformed into social rank in society at large. But prestige of rank in organizations may also conflict with professional prestige based on recognition by the scientific (or whatever) community, and this is a problem in research organizations.

The relationship of other attributes of office to rank are less straightforward. Job security and length of tenure (from one year contracts to lifetime contracts) tend to increase with rank, sharply in academic organizations with promotion to tenured associate professor in the U.S. or from Dozent to Professor in German universities. But presidents of American corporations may face greater risks of tenure (lightened by "Golden Parachutes" in the form of severance payments). Leisure is often a decreasing function of rank in business organizations and even vacation time need not increase with rank.

4.5 Rank and Precedence

For some purposes ranking in terms of equivalence classes under supervision (by counting the number of supervisory relationships) is not enough. Within each rank a further ordering is required resulting in a complete strict ordering, i.e., a ladder.

Examples
1. Order of succession in the government (president, vice president, senate majority leader, speaker of the house, secretary of state); also in corporations.
2. In the military: ranking officer (rank and seniority).
    German universities: rank and date of appointment to rank.

Precedence is partly honorific: who is the acting, i.e., ranking representative and recipient of honors accorded to the organization. It is operational in regard to succession to the presidency. Precedence supplements rank, it can never be contradictory to rank. It may be based on supplementary criteria such as

(i)   the actual number of persons under a person's control, the size of the control set;

(ii)   importance of area or department;

(iii)   seniority;

(iv)   merit, i.e., achievement.

Rank and precedence even when earned by merit, are basically ascriptive: once obtained they are held regardless of achievement.

Problems

1. Suppose the organization uses "Management (i.e., supervision) by Committee". Rewrite the rules for supervision.

2. Let the following rule apply in an organization: Every member with longer service (seniority) has authority over any member with shorter service. Is this an acyclic relationship? How would you change the postulates of supervision?

3. Consider an extended family forming a single household composed of the following members; yourself, a brother, a sister with husband and child, your parents, your father's brother, and your mother's sister and her sons. How would you assign "supervision" (or responsibility) so as to keep order in this household?

4. Draw the organization chart for the following assignment of
    supervisors.

i	1	2	3	4	5	6	7	8	9	10
sp (i)	7	10	9	9	7	9	11	7	10	11

5. For an organization with five members:
    a. find all organization charts (do not repeat identical
        charts);
    b. identify the balanced organizations;
    c. for the unbalanced organizations determine all possible
        rank assignments.

5 Distance

5.1 Organization Charts as Graphs

The organization chart serves not only as a description of the supervisory and control relationships but also as that of the official channels of communication. Communication is generally understood to be a two-way process so that there is no single direction attached to it. The organization chart is now to be treated as a graph rather than a digraph. In Chapter 5 the variable of interest is distance in organizations.

5.2 Communication Networks

In small organizations every member can have access to every other member without causing undue interference. However, in large organizations communications must go through "channels" for three basic reasons.

    (i)   It may not be known who is the right person to be contacted.

   (ii)   It is more efficient to bundle messages.

 (iii)   There would be too many messages.

The supervisory structure offers a natural communications network through which communications can be channelled and filtered so that the load of incoming messages is held at an acceptable level. In practice, the official channels are always supplemented by informal links through personal friendship by which the official path can be short circuited. Compared to the number of possible pairwise links, these unofficial links are not effective short cuts to path length for messages between members of higher ranks.

The following propositions are based on the supervisory structure as the official communications network.

Suppose that all direct communications are between supervisors and their immediate subordinates. Communications paths are obtained by stringing together such links between pairs of supervisor and subordinate.

Proposition 1: Between any two organization members i,j there exists a unique communication path such that each link in the path is traversed once and only once.

Remark: On any shortest path each point is traversed at most once.

Proof: Take the unique chain of command from i to the president and from j to the president and eliminate those portions that have been traversed twice.

N.B.: With informal links added to the communications network, there may be additional informal paths of shorter length.

Definition: The distance between two organization members i,j is the number of links on their unique communications path.

N.B.: In the union of the formal and informal communication networks distance is the minimal length of any paths from i to j.

N.B.: Distance is a norm:

1) $d_{ij} \geq 0$ and "=" only when $i = j$

2) $d_{ij} = d_{ji}$

3) $d_{ij} + d_{jk} \geq d_{ik}.$

Corollary: The distance between an organization member of rank r and an organization member of rank ρ is not larger than $2R - r - \rho.$

<u>Definition</u>: The height R of an organization is the length of the longest chain of command.

<u>Proposition 2</u>: In an organization of height R the diameter or largest distance is $\leq 2R$, and = if there are at least two disjoint chains of command of length R.
N.B.: In a balanced organization the diameter is 2R.

<u>Definition</u>: The excentricity of a point i in the organization is the largest distance from i to any member of the organization.

<u>Proposition 3</u>: In a balanced organization the eccentricity of any position of rank r is 2R − r.

<u>Definition</u>: A point of minimal eccentricity is called a center.

<u>Proposition 4</u>: A balanced organization has a unique center.

<u>Proof</u>: A tree of even diameter has a unique center, a tree of odd diameter has two adjacent centers. A balanced organization has an even diameter.

<u>Remark</u>: Suppose that in every given rank each supervisor has the same number of subordinates (quasi-regular organization). Then the center has the smallest average distance to all organization members.

As an alternative measure of closeness to members of the organization, the total or the average distance to organization members may be considered.

$$D(i) = \sum_{j} d(i,j) \quad \text{and} \tag{8}$$

$$\overline{d}(i) = \frac{1}{N-1} \sum_{j} d(i,j). \tag{9}$$

However, these are not necessarily minimized at a center, as the example of Figure 5.1 shows.

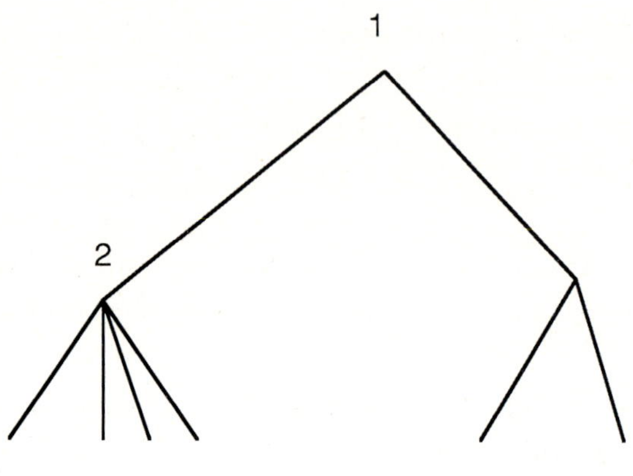

Figure 5.1.   Distances from Center are not Minimal

However, in a balanced organization with constant span of control in each rank, total and average distance are minimized at the center.

Example

Let   R   be the organization's radius, and   s   the uniform span of control.   Then

$$D(p) = \frac{s}{(s-1)^R} [Rs^{R+1} - (R+1)s^R + 1] \tag{10}$$

$$\overline{d}(p) = \frac{R\,s^{R+1} - (R+1)s^R + 1}{(s-1)(s^R - 1)} \tag{11}$$

and these values are the minimal ones for all points in the graph. $\overline{d}(p)$ is, in fact, independent of the presidential span of control.

Notice that (10) is an integer but (11) may be fractional.

For large R or s, $\overline{d}$ is approximated by

$$\overline{d}(p) = R - \frac{1}{s-1} \tag{12}$$

which shows that the minimum average distance is close to the radius, the maximal distance from the center, and closer the larger is s.

5.3 Locating the President

Suppose the connections between all departments in an organization are given in terms of an undirected organization chart specifying the communications network. We wish to assign the presidency to a suitable position using alternative objective functions.

Objective 1: For the president the maximal distance to any organization member shall be minimal.

In a graph, distance $d(i,j)$ between two points i,j is defined as the minimal number of edges separating the two vertices i,j (see p. 32).

Let $\ell(\pi,i,j)$ denote the length of a path π joining i and j.

Definition: Distance

$$d(i,j) = \underset{\pi}{\text{Min}}\ \ell(\pi,i,j).$$

The excentricity $\ell(i)$ of a vertex i is the largest distance between i and any point j in the graph.

Definition: $\ell(i) = \underset{j \varepsilon G}{\text{Max}}\ d(i,j)$.

A position of minimum excentricity is called a center c.

$$\ell(c) \leqslant \ell(i)$$

for all i ε G.

Theorem: The center of a tree consists of either a single point or of two adjacent points (Harary, Theorem 4.2, p. 35).

Thus either a single or two adjacent points will minimize the maximal distance to any organization member and are optimal locations for the presidency under objective 1.

In terms of distance, the counting up and counting down systems of rank assignment may be interpreted as follows:

Proposition: Counting up defines rank as distance from the farthest endpoint in any direction away from the center.

Counting down defines rank as radius R minus distance from the center.

Objective 2: Minimize the aggregate distance to all organization members.

$$D(i) = \sum_{j \varepsilon G} d(i,j).$$

The aggregate distance D(i) is bounded by

$$N-1 \leqslant D(i) \leqslant \sum_{i=1}^{N-1} i = \frac{N(N-1)}{2}.$$

The left alternative denotes a star, the right alternative a ladder.

<u>Proof:</u> by induction.

<u>Lemma:</u> For $N > 2$ distance assumes its minimum at an interior point (i.e., for a supervisory position).

The problem of locating the point of minimum aggregate distance is a special case of finding the Weber point of minimum transportation cost in a network, when all vertices generate one unit of freight to be transported to the plant location.

The Weber point w must satisfy the following necessary but not sufficient equilibrium condition:

On any branch from w the number of points cannot exceed one plus the number of points on all other branches combined.

$$1 + N_1 + N_{j-1} + N_{j+1} \,.. > N_j .$$

The increase in aggregate distance resulting from a shift of the presidency from w to an adjacent j is in fact

$$1 + \sum_{k \text{ adj } i} N_k - N_j > 0 .$$

Suppose all points have either

$$\text{degree } \sigma > 1 \quad \text{(interior point)}$$
$$\text{or} \quad \text{degree } \sigma = 1 \quad \text{(endpoint)}.$$

Then the center is also the point of minimum aggregate distance.

In fact, then we have a "quasi regular" organization in which the span of control is σ for the president and $\sigma - 1$ for all other supervisors.

5.4 Enumeration

The number of possible organizational charts rises rapidly with N. The number O_N of different organization charts with N members when all members are distinguished is equal to the number of labelled trees [Harary, 3, p. 179]

$$O_N = N^{N-2}.$$

The number of different organization charts with only the president identified is the number of unlabelled rooted trees (with root p). It is usually stated in terms of its counting series or generating function

$$T(x) = \sum_{N=1}^{\infty} T_N x^N$$

where T_N is the number of rooted trees with N elements. In principle, T_N may be found from Cayley's functional equation

$$T(x) = x \exp \sum_{n=1}^{\infty} T(x^n).$$

The following numbers are taken from [Harary, 3, p. 232]

N	3	4	5	6	7	8	9	10	15	11	
T_N	2	4	9	20	48	115	286	719	87,814	1,842	4,

N	20	25
T_N	12,826,228	2,067,174,645

Problem: Find all organization charts involving 3, 4 and 5 organization members.

II Perfect Management

6 Number of Positions

6.1 Span of Control

The relationship "supervision" is not one-to-one. By
Postulate 2 of Section 2, each organization member, except the
president, has one and only one supervisor. Supervision would
give rise to unnecessarily long chains of command, if a
supervisor had only one subordinate. The number of immediate
subordinates of a full-time supervisor is called his/her span of
control s. From now on this span is assumed to be at least 2,

$$s \geq 2.$$

Recommended values are given in the management literature [e.g.,
Koontz-O'Donnell, 1959]

$$3 \leq s < 8 \qquad \text{for supervising managers}$$

$$8 < s < 15 \qquad \text{for supervising operatives.}$$

The question of what determines the span of control and what
spans are optimal is discussed in Chapter III.

Without a bound on the span of control, organizations could
be made simple by appointing one member supervisor and all other
operatives.

In the graph representation of an organization--the
organization chart--each node has a degree defined as the number
of edges incident to this node. The degree is one for operatives

(located at endpoints); it equals the span of control for the president (the root). The span of control is the number of positions directly supervised by a supervisor. The degree equals one plus the span of control for nonpresidential supervisors (transit points). The degree indicates the number of persons to whom an immediate contact exists in the organization.

Thus, if the span of control s is equal for all supervisory positions, the node representing the president may be identified as the unique node of degree s, while all other transit points have degree $s+1$.

The graph representation of the supervisory (or control) structure of organization suggests that two types of imbalance may occur:

unequal length of chains of command and

uneven spans of control.

Other things equal a design is improved when a larger span of control is reduced by shifting a position so as to increase a smaller span of control. This is particularly apparent when the maximum span of control is thereby reduced.

An organization is called balanced when all its chains of command have equal length. This implies

1) The presidential position is the unique center of the organizational graph.
2) Rank assignments under counting up and counting down are equal.

While the potential or maximal span of control is a function of managerial capacity and supervisory requirements, the actual span may be governed by the principles of the division of the organization's task. Thus when a <u>territorial division</u> occurs the national market may be divided into three, four or six major regions, each of which is in turn divided into a number of sub-regions. The nesting of regions may be governed by geographic rather than managerial considerations. Christaller has suggested nesting factors of 2, 3, 4 and 6 or maximally 7.

6.2 Quantification of Task

Organizations exist for some purpose. This may involve many disparate tasks. For purpose of economic analysis the size of the task can be described in person units. If necessary these can be further reduced to some standard measure of person performance, i.e., to efficiency units.

The task size Q of an organization may be given and fixed, or it may be chosen by the organization. Conversely, the size N of the organization (in person units) may be given or chosen.

The following scenarios arise:

	N fixed	N chosen
Q fixed	1	2
Q chosen	3	4

Table 6.1. Size and Task

1. Both task and size are prescribed. No choice. The only question is: are the resources N adequate for the task Q?

2. For a given task Q the organization may choose its size. What is the minimum size N required? What is the maximal size N that may be chosen?

3. With fixed resources, the organization may determine the size of its task. What is the maximal, what is the minimal choice?

4. What objective should be pursued when both task size and organization size may be chosen by the organization?

Well defined objectives may be set in every case when <u>efficiency</u> is the goal.

2. Find the minimal N for a given Q.

3. Find the maximal Q for a given N.

4. Maximize $\frac{Q}{N}$ the average product or minimize $\frac{N}{Q}$ the average cost.

(N.B.: Returns and costs are measured in person units only. For money costs, cf. Chapter 10.)

In this chapter we investigate efficient solutions to problem 2. Rather than in terms of N, the problem may be stated in terms of $M = N-Q$, the total amount of supervision, i.e., non-operative labor.

"Minimize supervision M for a fixed size of task Q when a uniform span of control s applies throughout the organization."

6.3 Constant Span of Control

In the Sections 6.1-6.5 we consider organizations with constant span of control s. This is interpreted to mean that any organization member can supervise at most s other organization members. If he/she supervises

$$m < s$$

members, then he/she can perform an amount $\frac{s-m}{s}$ of operative work. (All work is measured in person units, assumed to be equal for all organization members.) Such a person would do both supervision and operative work.

To begin with we shall allow part-time employment as well. The total amount of work any particular person can be hired to do is then ≤ 1.

Let the task of the organization be given and consist of Q person units of operative work. We ask:

What is the minimum amount of total supervisory work required by Q units of operative work?

What is the minimum size of the organization and how does it depend on the organizational design, i.e., the way in which operative and supervisory work are allocated and supervisory relationships are arranged?

Our principal result is the following:

Theorem 1

Let the span of control s and the size of the task Q be given. Then the required amount of supervision M is uniquely determined and independent of organizational design

$$M = \frac{Q-1}{s-1} \tag{1}$$

Corollary 2

The size of the organization is determined by

$$N = \frac{sQ-1}{s-1} \tag{2}$$

Proof: The total number of organization members is $M + Q$, but only $M + Q - 1$ require supervision. The number of supervisors required (including the president) is therefore

$$M = \frac{1}{s} (M + Q - 1)$$

Solving for M yields

$$M = \frac{Q-1}{s-1} \tag{1}$$

The number of supervisors is thus a linear function of the number of operatives Q. For large organizations $1 \ll Q$ so that approximately

$$M \doteq \frac{Q}{s-1} \tag{3}$$

Each operative gives rise to an administrative force totalling

$$\frac{1}{s} + \frac{1}{s^2} + \frac{1}{s^3} + \ldots = \frac{1}{s-1}.$$

The fact that the president needs no supervision actually terminates this chain after at most R steps, and this results in the corrective term $\frac{-1/Q}{s-1}$ in (1) omitted from (3). From (1), the size of the organization is obtained by considering

$$N = Q + M$$

$$N = \frac{sQ-1}{s-1}$$

using (1).

For a large organization we may approximate (2) by

$$N \doteq \frac{Q}{1 - \frac{1}{s}}. \tag{4}$$

The factor $\dfrac{1}{1 - \frac{1}{s}}$ is sometimes called the <u>organizational multiplier</u>. It shows the total employment generated in an organization by one unit of outside work Q. The organizational multiplier is sensitive to s when s is small. Thus using a span of control $s = 3$ when $s = 4$ would have been adequate increases the size of the organization by a factor

$$\frac{1}{1 - \frac{1}{3}} - \frac{1}{1 - \frac{1}{4}} = \frac{3}{2} - \frac{4}{3} = \frac{1}{6}$$

Further corollaries of (1) are

$$Q = 1 + (s-1)M \tag{5}$$

The amount of work that can be supervised by means of a given
management force M is a linear increasing function of M with
slope $s-1$.

$$Q = \frac{1}{s} + \frac{s-1}{s} N$$

The total output that can be produced by an organization of
size N is thus a linear increasing function of N with slope
$1 - \frac{1}{s}$

$$M = \frac{1}{s} (N-1) \tag{6}$$

The total management required is an increasing linear function of
the organization's size with slope $\frac{1}{s}$.

$$N = 1 + sM. \tag{7}$$

The size of the organization is one plus s times the size of
management.

The fact that the total requirement of supervision should be
independent of organizational design is surprising. In Figure
6.1 we compare all following possibilities of organizing of
supervision $Q = 3$ and $s = 3$. The amount of operative work
done by each organization member is listed in parentheses.

Notice also: The number of supervisory relationships is
$N-1$. This follows since N is the number of vertices and $N-1$
the number of edges in a tree. Hence, the number of supervisory
relationships is also uniquely determined by s and Q.

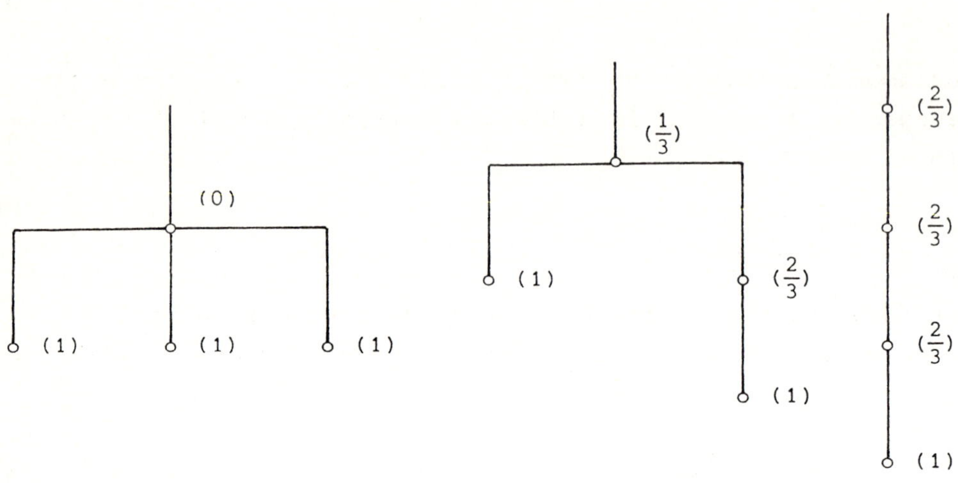

Figure 6.1. Organizational Designs
for Q = 3, s = 3

6.4 Disaggregation of Task

Consider an organization whose workload is not fixed, e.g.,
because tasks arrive at random and are disposed of or join a
queue. At times of slack, operatives and supervisors will do
jobs required for the maintenance of the organization so that
there is a positive opportunity cost of using the organization's
personnel.

In this section we ask: how much managerial work M_j is
generated by a job j of size Q_j?

Suppose job j engages an amount p_j of the president's time. Then, as above

$$M_j = \frac{1}{s}(Q_j + M_j - p_j)$$

or

$$M_j = \frac{Q_j - p_j}{s-1} \tag{1}$$

This is the disaggregated version of (6.3.1). Summing over j yields the total managerial effort required.

$$M = \sum_i M_j = \sum_j \frac{Q_j - p_j}{s-1}$$

$$= \frac{Q - \sum p_j}{s-1}$$

$$M \geq \frac{Q-1}{s-1} \tag{2}$$

in view of the constraint on presidential time

$$\sum_j p_j \leq 1 \tag{3}$$

From (2) it is now seen that (6.3.1) represents the minimum of managerial effort in an organization that will be achieved only by utilizing the president fully in the ultimate supervision of the various tasks of the organization.

Now p_j is not given but results from an economic choice. Concretely, given the job Q_j and hence the total work load Q for the organization, the constraint (3) requires that R be chosen sufficiently high, as will now be shown.

Consider first p_j for a particular job Q_j. Inspection of the organizational chart shows the following. First, assume that $Q_j \leq 1$. Let d_j be the number of supervisory relationship between the operators performing j and the president (or the distance of this operative from the president). Then clearly

$$p_j = Q_j \cdot (\frac{1}{s})^{d_j} \tag{4}$$

From (4) it follows that for individual jobs j, the amount of managerial effort required does depend on organizational structure. For substituting (4) in (1) yields

$$M_j = \frac{Q_j}{s-1} \cdot [1-s^{-d_j}] \tag{5}$$

Hence, the length of the chain of command d_j determines the amount of managerial effort required. As one might expect, this effort increases with the length of the chain, although the increase becomes small when d_j is large.

Formula (4) is valid also when several operatives work on j provided they all have the same distance from the president.

Suppose next that the organization is balanced and that all operatives have rank zero. Then all operatives have the same distance $d = R$ from the president. Hence

$$p_j = Q_j \cdot s^{-R} \tag{4a}$$

Aggregating over jobs yields

$$s^{-R}Q = s^{-R} \sum_j Q_j = \sum_j s^{-R}Q_j = \sum_j p_j \leq 1$$

using (3) or

$$Q \leq s^R \tag{6}$$

Equation (6) determines the minimum height of the organization.

$$R \geq \frac{\log Q}{\log s} \qquad (6a)$$

When the organization is not balanced, the distance from the president may vary among the operatives charged with task j. The length of the longest chain then determines the marginal cost (in person units) of administration generated by an unit increase in job j.

An interesting implication of (2) is that the minimal amount of managerial effort (and hence of total effort) generated in the organization by a task totalling Q is always the same, provided the president is fully utilized. Hence, the minimal effect is achieved merely by making full use of the president's capacity.

This may be illustrated by calculating the minimal work load for various ranks in an organization with R ranks and given s.

<u>Problem</u>: For $s = 3$, $R = 2$ show the work load for each rank as Q varies from 0 to 9.

	$0 \leqslant Q \leqslant 1$	$1 \leqslant Q \leqslant 3$	$3 \leqslant Q \leqslant 9$	$9 \leqslant Q \leqslant 27$
m_3	0	$\frac{(Q-1)}{2}$	1	1
m_2	0	0	$\frac{Q-3}{2}$	3
m_1	0	0	0	$\frac{Q-9}{2}$

Table 6.2. Solution

6.5 Full-Time Assignments

So far, fractional (i.e., part-time) employment was admitted as well as a splitting of time between operative and supervisory roles. In this section we examine the implications of full-time assignments to supervisory and operative work.

<u>Lemma</u>: Full-time management is possible if and only if operative work requires an integer number of operatives, Q and $s-1$ divides $Q-1$

$$s-1 \mid sQ-1 \tag{1}$$

<u>Proof</u>: Equation (6.3.1)

It follows that organizational size $N = M + Q$ is then also integer, in fact

$$N = \left\{\frac{sQ-1}{s-1}\right\} = \left\{Q + \frac{Q-1}{s-1}\right\} = Q + \left\{\frac{Q-1}{s-1}\right\}. \tag{2}$$

Here $\{x\}$ = smallest integer $\geq x$.

<u>Corollary</u>: $N = \dfrac{sQ-1}{s-1}$

is integer if and only if $\dfrac{Q-1}{s-1}$ is integer.

<u>Corollary 2</u>: Let s, Q, N be integers. Then

$$s-1 \mid Q-1 \quad \text{if and only if} \quad s \mid N-1$$

<u>Proof</u>:

$$M = \frac{Q-1}{s-1} \tag{3}$$

is integer if and only if $s-1 \mid Q-1$. Also from (6.3.7)

$$M = \frac{1}{s}(N-1) \tag{4}$$

Thus M is integer if and only if $s \mid N-1$.
Combining (3) and (4) completes the proof. $\|$

Why is full-time supervision or management advantageous?
One important reason is the advantage of specialization, or the
famous division of labor.

"The greatest improvement in the productive powers of
labour, and the greater part of the skill, dexterity, and
judgment with which it is any where directed, or applied, seem to
have been the effects of the division of labour...

This great increase of the quantity of work, which, in
consequence of the division of labour, the same number of people
are capable of performing, is owing to three different
circumstances; first, to the increase of dexterity in every
particular workman; secondly, to the saving of the time which is
commonly lost in passing from one species of work to another; and
lastly, to the invention of a great number of machines which
facilitate and abridge labour, and enable one man to do the work
of many... (and) every man to apply himself to a particular
occupation, and to cultivate and bring to perfection whatever
talent or genius he may possess for that particular species of
business" (Adam Smith, pp. 3, 7, 15).

There is, however, another reason, perhaps even more
important, for organizations to make management a full-time
occupation. Any part-time assignment of operative work to
managers results in a lengthening of some chain of command due to
the reduction in the span of control. More precisely

Proposition

Suppose $s-1 | Q-1$. Any assignment of operative work to a
supervisor lengthens a chain of command, while keeping the number
of positions constant.

Example:

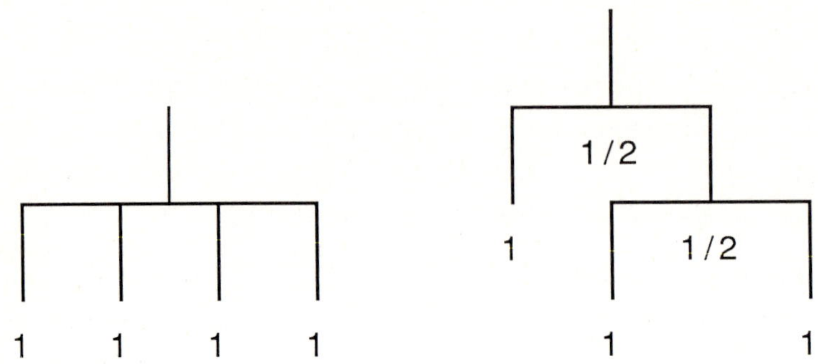

Figure 6.2. Allocation of Operative Work, s = 4

Full-time supervision will be called <u>management</u>. In an organization with division of labor on a full-time basis there are thus two specialized types of members: operatives and managers. (Sometimes the operatives may be divided into those performing the task of the organization and support personnel, Section 8.6.)

Max Weber (1929) has pointed out that all hierarchically structured organizations (bureaucracies) are run by managers whose functions are broadly similar, whether they manage government bureaus (civil servants), corporate business firms (executives), churches (clerics), armies (officers), political parties, labor unions, hospitals or other modern organizations (functionaries).

When (1) is violated, full-time hiring implies an organization of size

$$N \;=\; \left\{ \frac{sQ-1}{s-1} \right\} \tag{2}$$

The number of full-time supervisors is then equal to

$$M \;=\; \left\{ \frac{Q-1}{s-1} \right\} \tag{3}$$

6.6 Supervisory Load and Effort

In some organizations the span of control may be determined
not by long-run considerations of efficient organizational design
but dictated by the numbers of operatives Q and managers M,
available in the short run.

The total supervisory load will be defined as the number of
persons in the organization requiring supervision. If members
are either operatives or managers, the total supervisory load may
be written also as

$$M + Q - 1.$$

Let the managers be numbered $j = 1, \ldots, M$ and let s_j be
manager j's span of control. This span of control is also this
manager's portion of the total supervisory load. In other words
adding the amounts s_j of supervision contributed by managers
j yields the total supervisory load

$$\sum_{j=1}^{M} s_j = M + Q - 1$$

or

$$\sum_{j=1}^{M} (s_j - 1) = Q - 1. \tag{1}$$

Proposition 1: The number of operatives minus one equals the sum
of the spans of control minus one.

When all spans are equal this becomes

$$M \cdot (s-1) = Q-1$$

or, once more

$$M = \frac{Q-1}{s-1} \tag{6.3.1}$$

For M to be an integer one must assume, that

$$s-1 \mid Q-1. \tag{2}$$

Notice, however, that (1) is valid regardless of divisibility assumptions.

One implication of (1) is the following: A unit increase in the labor force (operatives) requires a unit increase in some manager's span of control unless the number of managers is changed.

Suppose s is not integer. Then some manager(s) must do some operative work unless supervision of the same operative may be shared.

Another implication of (1) is the following: Suppose that a manager is added with span of control s. Then his/her net contribution to the total supervisory load is s-1. This means that s-1 persons can be removed from the spans of control of other managers.

6.7 Allocation of Managers in the Short Run

Let now Q and M be given. What is the required span of control in this organization?

Solving equation (2) for s

$$s = 1 + \frac{Q-1}{M}. \tag{1}$$

<u>Proposition 2</u>: Let $M \mid Q-1$ then a uniform span of control s can be applied throughout the organization where s is given by equation (1).

What happens when Q-1 is not divisible by M? The choice of control spans that comes closest to a uniform span is then the following.

<u>Proposition 3</u>:   Let

$$Q-1 = \sigma M + k \qquad 0 \leqslant k < \sigma \tag{2}$$

or

$$\left[\frac{Q-1}{M}\right] = \sigma \qquad k = (Q-1) \bmod M. \tag{3}$$

Then the most even distribution of the total supervisory load is achieved when

$$k \quad \text{managers have span of control} \quad s_i = \sigma+1$$
$$\tag{4}$$
$$M-k \quad \text{managers have span of control} \quad s_i = \sigma$$

<u>Proof</u>: $k(\sigma+1) + (M-k)\sigma = k + M\sigma = Q-1$ by (2).

Supervision of operatives is not the same job as supervising other supervisors. Suppose the span of control in supervising operatives is fixed at s_1. What is the resulting span for controlling managers?

Let us denote operators by L. To simplify somewhat assume $s_1 \mid L$ then there is a total of

$$m_1 = \frac{L}{s_1} \tag{5}$$

first line supervisors, i.e., supervisors of operatives. Setting $m_1 = Q$ we may then apply the previous analysis. In other words, we are now concerned with a hierarchy of managers only, the first line managers playing the same role as operatives before.

6.8   Average Span of Control and Output

In this and the following section, span of control is not constant but a function of rank (cf. Starbuck, 1964)

$$s_r \qquad\qquad r = 1, \ldots, R.$$

Here r is the rank of the supervisor and s_r the number of persons under his/her immediate supervision.

We consider an organization for which an average span of control $\bar{s}$ is given

$$\bar{s} = \frac{1}{R} \sum_{r=1}^{R} s_r \tag{1}$$

We ask: Which distribution of spans of control among ranks results in the largest output, i.e., a maximum number of operatives.

$$\underset{s_r}{\mathrm{Max}} \ \prod_{r=1}^{R} s_r \tag{2}$$

subject to (1).

<u>Proposition</u>: For a given average span of control, output is maximized when all spans of control are equal.

<u>Proof</u>: The well-known inequality for the arithmetic and geometric mean (Beckenbach and Bellman, 1961) states that

$$\sqrt[R]{\prod_{r=1}^{R} s_r} \ \leq \ \frac{\sum_{r=1}^{R} s_r}{R} \tag{3}$$

and "=" if and only if all $s_r \equiv s$.

Taking the Rth power in (3) proves the assertion. $\|$

This shows one advantage of constant spans of control: it permits the largest possible output from an organization. This point is further explored in Chapter 9 on Regular Organizations.

6.9 Spans of Control Decreasing with Rank

In this section we study situations where the ideal or intended span of control depends on rank r. Specifically let it be a non-increasing function of rank. To compare organizations of different size but similar spans of control we specify that

$$s_r = \sigma_{R-r} \tag{1}$$

The span of control for managers in rank r is a given number σ_{R-r} <u>depending on the distance from the president</u> R-r.

Two variables of interest are n_r and N_r.

$$n_r = \prod_{i=r+1}^{R} s_i = \prod_{i=r+1}^{R} \sigma_{R-i} \tag{2}$$

$$N_r = \sum_{j=r}^{R} n_j = \sum_{j=r}^{R} \prod_{i=j+1}^{R} \sigma_{R-i} \tag{3}$$

Our basic assumption is

$$\sigma_1 > \sigma_0$$
$$\qquad\qquad i = 1, \ldots, R-1 \tag{4}$$
$$\sigma_{i+1} \geqslant \sigma_i$$

This hypothesis is in agreement with empirical findings (Starbuck 1964). Suppose the organization is balanced. We consider the following ratio

$$a_{R-r} = \frac{N_{r+1}}{n_r} \tag{5}$$

This ratio measures the amount of supervision or administrative effort (in person units) generated in ranks r+1, ..., R by personnel in rank r. Notice that assumption (1) makes this ratio a function of R-r. Consider in particular

$$a_R = \frac{N_1}{n_0} = \frac{M}{Q} \qquad (5a)$$

measuring management per operative or administrative effort per unit of output.

Now a_R tells us how administrative effort per unit of output varies with the height R (a measure of size) of the organization.

We observe that the a_R satisfy a recursive equation

$$a_{R+1} = \frac{a_R \cdot n_0 + n_0}{n_0 \cdot \sigma_R}$$

or

$$a_{R+1} = \frac{1 + a_R}{\sigma_R} \qquad (6)$$

In particular, when $\sigma_r = s$

$$a_{R+1} = \frac{1 + a_R}{s}$$

approaches the limit

$$a = \frac{1+a}{s} \qquad a = \frac{1}{s-1}$$

in agreement with (6.3.3).

What are the implications of (4)? We show

<u>Lemma:</u> Assume

$$\sigma_0 < \sigma_1 \leqslant \sigma_2 \leqslant \ldots \leqslant \sigma_R - 1 \qquad (4)$$

then

$$\frac{1}{\sigma_R - 1} \leqslant a_{R+1} \leqslant \frac{1}{\sigma_0} \tag{7}$$

The proof is given in Appendix C.

The results of the lemma may be strengthened in form of the following

Theorem 1: Let $\sigma_0 < \sigma_1 \leq \sigma_2 \leq \cdots \leq \sigma_{R-1}$ then a_R, the ratio of managers to operatives in an organization with R ranks, is a monotone non-increasing function of R. a_R is constant if and only if

$$\sigma_r = \sigma_0 + 1 \qquad r = 1, \ldots, R-1 \tag{4a}$$

yielding

$$a_R = \frac{1}{\sigma_0}.$$

Proof: Consider $a_{R+1} - a_R =$

$$= \frac{1 + a_R}{\sigma_R} - a_R = \frac{1 - a_R(\sigma_R - 1)}{\sigma_R} \leq 0$$

since $a_R \geq \frac{1}{\sigma_{R-1} - 1} \geq \frac{1}{\sigma_{R-1}}$ by (6).

This proves that a_R is monotone non-increasing.

Now $a_{R+1} = a_R$ if and only if

$$a_R = \frac{1}{\sigma_R - 1} \quad \text{and} \quad \sigma_R = \sigma_{R-1}.$$

Thus $\qquad \sigma_R = \sigma_1 \qquad$ and

$$a_R = \frac{1}{\sigma_1 - 1} = \text{constant.} \tag{8}$$

Specifically now for $R = 1$

$$a_1 = \frac{1}{\sigma_0}.$$

This equals (7) if and only if $\sigma_0 + 1 = \sigma_1$. $\qquad \|$

The economic content of the theorem is the following. A decrease in the span of control with rank implies constant or increasing returns to scale in administration as measured by the ratio of administrators to operatives. Constant returns to scale apply if and only if the common span of control exceeds that of the president by one.

These results may be generalized by altering the span of control of the lowest level of administrators (foremen) to be an arbitrary multiple k of the constant span s at higher levels. The ratio of administrators to workers is then just $\frac{1}{k}$ times the previously calculated a_k.

7 Estimation

The actual span of control can always be read off an
organizational chart. Suppose, however, only the numbers of
positions of various ranks n_r are given. In this case a lower
bound on the average span of control may be inferred. If more
information is given, e.g., that the organization is balanced,
more precise estimates are available.

7.1 From M and Q

Suppose first that all supervisors and all operatives can be
identified. Then M and Q are known. From (5.1)

$$(s-1)M = Q-1 = N-M-1$$

$$s = \frac{N-1}{M} \tag{1}$$

This relationship $s = \frac{N-1}{M}$ derived for constant spans of
control s defines an average span of control in the case of
unequal s_i. The numerator tells the number of persons to be
supervised and the denominator the number of persons doing the
supervision. Supervisors and operatives are clearly identified,
for instance, when all persons of rank r* or lower are
operatives and all persons of rank r* are supervisors. In this
case

$$M = N_{r*+1}$$

Here N_r is defined as

$$N_r = \sum_{i=r}^{R} n_i$$

7.2 From Lists of Positions by Rank

We consider next the case where only a set containing the supervisors is known.

Theorem: Let G be a subset of members of an organization and let H contain the set M of all supervisors of G. Then

$$s \geq \frac{|G| - 1}{|H|} \tag{2}$$

Proof:

$$|M| = \frac{1}{s}(|G| - 1)$$

if G contains the president and the members of M supervise no persons not belonging to M. Otherwise,

$$|M| > \frac{1}{s}(|G| - 1).$$

Combining the inequality and equation yields

$$s \geq \frac{|G| - 1}{|M|} \geq \frac{|G| - 1}{|H|} \quad \text{since} \quad M \subset H.$$

Application: Let G = set of persons of rank $\geq r$

$$|G| = N_r = n_r + n_{r+1} + \ldots + n_{R-1} + n_R$$

H = set of persons of rank $\geq r+1$

$$|H| = N_{r+1}.$$

Then

$$\hat{s}(r) \geq \frac{N_r - 1}{N_{r+1}} \tag{3}$$

where $\hat{s}(r)$ denotes the average span of control of supervisors above rank r.

What is the smallest integer span of control $\hat{s}$ consistent with position plan n_r, $r = 0, \ldots, R$ of the organization? From (3) we infer

$$\hat{s} = \underset{r=0,\ldots,R-1}{\text{Max}} \left\{ \frac{N_r - 1}{N_{r+1}} \right\} \tag{4}$$

As an example consider the Library of Congress.

n_r	N_r	$s(r)$
1	1	
1	2	1
1	3	1
7	10	3
3	13	1.2
9	22	1.6
45	67	3
57	124	1.8
188	312	2.5
218	530	1.7
322	852	1.6
616	1468	1.7

Table 7.1. Library of Congress (The Budget, 1982)

The estimated span of control at levels GS 18 and higher is $s = 3$.

Suppose it is known that all positions above a certain rank r^* are full-time supervisors and that the span of control is constant. Then the estimate (3) is exact and r^* is determined as the maximizer in (3).

r	n_r	N_r	$\hat{s}(r)$
Exec II	1	1	
Exec III 1	2	2	
ES 6	9	11	5
5	6	17	1.46
4	65	82	4.76
3	4	86	1.03

Table 7.2. Office of Management and Budget (The Budget, 1982)

The estimated span of control is 5. It applies at the two upper levels. The second estimate 4.76 is close enough to permit the inference, that $r^* = $ ES 4 so that all personnel above this rank is purely supervisory.

Actually, by promoting x persons from rank ES4 to rank ES5 and y persons from rank ES6 to Exec III, the required span of control in the Office of Management and the Budget can be reduced to s = 4. This is shown in Table 7.3.

r	n_r	N_r	$\hat{s}(r) = \dfrac{N_{r-1}^{-1}}{N_r}$	n'_r	N'_r	$\hat{s}$
Exec II	1	1	1	1	1	$1+x$
Exec III	1	2	5	$1+x$	$2+x$	$\dfrac{10}{2+x} \leqq 4$
ES6	9	11	1.45	$9-x$	11	$\dfrac{16+y}{11} \leqslant 4$
ES5	6	17	4.76	$6+y$	$17+y$	$\dfrac{81}{17+y} \leqq 4$
ES4	65	82	1.04	$65-y$	82	1.04
ES3	4	86		4	86	

Table 7.3. Reduction of Span of Control by Promotion

$$\frac{10}{2+x} \leqq 4 \quad \text{is achieved by} \quad x = 1, \quad n'_4 = 3$$

$$\frac{16+y}{11} \leqslant 4 \quad \text{and} \quad \frac{81}{17+y} \leqslant 4 \quad \text{is achieved by} \quad 4 \leqslant y \leqslant 28. \quad \text{Let}$$

$$y = 4, \quad n'_2 = 21.$$

It is possible also to lower the span of control by demoting some persons. But this is only of academic interest.

7.3 Other Estimates

In a balanced organization, the supervisors of personnel in rank r are all found in rank $r+1$. Therefore, the average span of control for supervisors of rank r is

$$s_r = \frac{n_{r-1}}{n_r} \qquad r = 1, \ldots, R. \tag{7}$$

An average span of control for the entire organization may be estimated as the geometric mean of (7).

$$\hat{s} = \sqrt[R]{s_1 \cdot s_2 \cdots s_R}$$

$$= \sqrt[R]{\frac{n_0}{n_1} \cdot \frac{n_1}{n_2} \cdot \cdots \frac{n_{R-1}}{1}}$$

$$\hat{s} = \sqrt[R]{n_0} \tag{8}$$

This estimate is simply the Rth root of the number of operatives. An example is the German Army (Reichswehr) in 1933 (Table 7.4).

Estimate (8) assumes in fact that the balanced organization is regular, i.e., has the same span of control throughout.

When n_0 is unknown, but N and R are given, then

$$1 + s + \ldots + s^R = N$$

$$\frac{s^{R+1} - 1}{s-1} = N \tag{9}$$

An estimate $\hat{s}$ may be obtained from (9) through

iteration

$$s_{(n+1)} = [1 + (s_{(n)}-1)N]^{\frac{1}{R+1}}$$

or approximately

$$s_{(n+1)} = [(s_{(n)}-1)N]^{\frac{1}{R+1}} \tag{9a}$$

In a nonbalanced organization not all operative positions are in rank zero. The span of control is then underestimated by (8).

Return to (7.2.2) A sharper bound for s can be found by eliminating from H all non-supervisory personnel. Let M_r denote supervisors of rank r and above. Then

$$\hat{s}(r) = \left\{\frac{N_r - 1}{M_{r+1}}\right\}. \tag{10}$$

which is a sharper estimate than (3).

Examples are given in Tables 7.6 and 7.7.

Rank	Number of Positions per Unit	Title
9	1	Chef der Heeresleitung
8	2	Oberbefehlshaber
7	4 (6)	Divisionskommandeur
6	2	Infantrie und Artilleriefuhrer
5	4	Regimentskommandeure + 5 Batalions und Abteilungskommandeure
4	4	Batallionskommandeure + 1 Kompaniechef
3	4	Kompaniechef
2	3	Zugführer
1	3	Gruppenfuhrer
0	15	Mann

Total number: $n_0 = 100,000$ men

Average span of control $\hat{s} = \sqrt[9]{100,000} = 3.5938 \approx 3.5$

Source: von Matuschka, Edgar Graf, <u>Organisation des Reichsheeres in Handbuch zur Deutschen Militargeschichte 1648-1939</u> (Hans Meier-Welcker und Wolfgang von Groote, eds.), Vol. VI (1970), 305-379, Frankfurt: Bernhard und Graefe.

Table 7.4. Reichswehr

Rank	Title	Number
0	Research Associate	430
1	Project Leader	
2	Group Leader	
3	Department Head	
4	Division Chief	
5	Research Director	3
6	Executive Director	1

Calculated average span of control

$$\hat{s} = \sqrt[6]{430} = 2.74$$

Table 7.5. Research Organizations in Bavaria

Rank	Responsibility	Title
12	Oberster Kriegsherr	Kaiser
11	Oberste Heeresleitung	Feldmarschall
10	Heeresgruppe	Generaloberst
9	Armeeoberkommando	General
8	Armeekorps	Generalleutnant
7	Division	Generalmajor
6	Brigade	Oberst
5	Regiment	Oberstleutnant
4	Batalion	Major
3	Kompanie	Hauptmann
2	Zug	Leutnant, Oberleutnant
1	Gruppe	Feldwebel, Unteroffizier
0	Soldat	Gefreiter, Schütze
Total number at mobilization		3,822,000
Average span of control		3.44

Source: Cron, Hermann, <u>Die Organisation des Deutschen Heeres im Weltkrieg</u>, Berlin, 1923: Mittler und Sohn.

Table 7.6. German Army World War I

10	General of the Army
9	Group Commander
8	Area Commander
7	Division Commander
6	Brigade Commander
5	Regimental Commander
4	Batallion Commander
3	Company Chief
2	Platoon Leader
1	Group Leader

782,000 men

Average span of control: 3.77

Table 7.7. U.S. Army, 1977

8 Assignment

<u>8.1   The Problem of Implementation</u>

Fractional task sizes may be allocated, starting at the president's level in order to make full use of presidential capacity. Thus when

$$1 < Q \leqslant s$$

the president is assigned an amount x of operative work such that

$$s(1-x) \qquad = \quad Q-x$$

$$\text{operatives supervised} = \text{operatives hired}$$

$$x = \frac{s-Q}{s-1}$$

Now let

$$s^{R-1} < Q \leqslant s^{R}$$

One possible assignment is the following: Assign s^{R-r} persons to rank r, $r = 1, \ldots, R$. Assign an amount x of operative work to first line supervisors of rank 1. The number of operatives in rank zero is then given by

$$n_0 = Q-x = s(s^{R-1} - x)$$

from which

$$x = \frac{s^R - Q}{s-1}$$

Generalizing (1). In either case operative work is handled at the lowest possible levels. Now turn to the problem of full-time, i.e., integer assignments.

8.2 Integer Assignments

Can the supervisory requirements always be implemented without slack? In particular, when Q is integer and

$$s-1 \mid Q-1 \tag{1}$$

how can one design an organizational structure composed of full-time operatives and full-time managers as supervisors?

There are, in fact, many designs which implement (6.3.1). In fact, there are as many as there are trees with the properties mentioned above: having Q endpoints, one internal point of degree s and all other internal points of degree s+1. (See Section 6.1 above.)

One simple way of assigning persons to full-time management or operative work is as follows.

$$s-1 \mid Q-1$$

means

$$Q = 1 + k \cdot (s-1)$$

for some integer k. When k = 1, we have a simple organization. Suppose we have constructed an organization chart for some k. Then making one operative a supervisor and assigning s additional subordinates to him generates an organization chart for k+1 with full-time assignments. If the operative made supervisor has minimal rank, the result is an s-ladder (Figure 10.1). It produces an assignment with maximal ranks.

8.3 Minimizing Ranks

To obtain an assignment with minimal rank we proceed as follows. All Q operatives are given rank zero and a maximum number of supervisors is assigned to these and given rank one. The number of supervisors of rank one is then equal to

$$\left[\frac{Q}{s}\right] = n_1 \tag{1}$$

where $[x]$ = largest integer $\leq x$.

This leaves $Q - s\left[\dfrac{Q}{s}\right] = o_1$
positions unsupervised.

Next, we determine a maximum number of supervisors of rank 2

$$\left[\frac{n_1 + o_1}{s}\right] = n_2 \tag{2}$$

write

$$n_1 + o_1 = s\left[\frac{n_1 + k_1}{s}\right] + o_2 \tag{3}$$

so that o_2 are now unsupervised positions.
In general, let

$$n_{r+1} = \left[\frac{n_r + o_r}{s}\right] \tag{4}$$

$$o_{r+1} = n_r + o_r - s n_{r+1} \tag{5}$$

This can be continued until $n_R = 1$, $o_R = 0$.

It is easy to show that $n_r + o_r$ and hence n_{r+1} decrease with r as long as $n_{r+1} > 1$.

Moreover, one shows by induction that

$$s-1 \mid (n_r + o_r - 1)$$

for all positive values of the parenthesis. From these two facts it follows that eventually

$$n_R = 1 \quad \text{and} \quad o_R = 0.$$

It is clear that this algorithm produces a rank assignment by "counting-up" and that the resulting numbers of positions at each level and thus the design are unique.

Since the number of positions falls by at most $\frac{1}{s}$ as one moves up, it follows once more that

$$Q \leq s^R \qquad \text{or}$$

$$R \geq \frac{\log Q}{\log s} \tag{6}$$

When condition (1) is not satisfied, i.e., $s-1$ does not divide $Q-1$, then in order to apply the algorithm one adds as many positions in rank zero (at most $s-2$) so that condition (1), the divisibility requirement, holds. These positions will be deleted once more when the algorithm is finished. This results in a rank minimizing assignment.

<u>Example</u>: Office of Management and the Budget (data from Table 7.2)

From $s = 5$, $N = 86$ one obtains $Q = \frac{1}{5} + \frac{4}{5} \cdot 86 = 69$
which equals the number of positions in ranks ES3 and ES4. Suppose
all operatives are promoted to rank ES4.

r		n_r	o_r
3	EXEC III	$[\frac{3+2}{5}] = 1$	0
2	ES6	$[\frac{13-4}{5}] = 3$	2
1	ES5	$[\frac{69}{5}] = 13$	4
0	ES4	69	0

Table 8.1. Office of Management and the Budget Restructured

Even after promoting all operatives to rank ES4, this agency could
be managed by eliminating the top rank and assigning more persons to
rank ES5. The result is fewer positions in ranks above ES5.

When operatives hold ranks above the minimum rank zero and
q_r $r = 0,1, \ldots$ denotes the number of operatives in ranks r the
algorithm still applies with the obvious modifications

$$n_{r+1} = q_{r+1} + [\frac{n_r + o_r}{s}] \qquad (4a)$$

$$o_{r+1} = n_r + o_r - s \cdot n_{r+1} \qquad (7)$$

Example: Library of Congress.

A roll of $N = 1468$ members and span of control $s = 3$ imply

$$Q = \frac{1}{3} + \frac{2}{3} \, 1468 = 979$$

operatives. Let these be assigned as follows

$$q_2 = 41$$
$$q_1 = 322$$
$$q_0 = 616$$

r	q_r	n_r	o_r
7		$[\frac{3}{3}] = 1$	
6		$[\frac{8+1}{3}] = 3$	0
5		$[\frac{24+1}{3}] = 8$	1
4		$[\frac{72+1}{3}] = 24$	1
3		$[\frac{217}{3}] = 72$	1
2	41	$41 + [\frac{527+1}{3}] = 217$	0
1	322	$322 + [\frac{616}{3}] = 527$	1
0	616	616	

Table 8.2.   Library of Congress Restructured

r	0	1	2	3	4	5	6	$\geqslant 7$
Actual	616	322	218	188	57	45	9	12
Reassigned	616	527	217	72	24	8	3	1

Table 8.3.   Comparison of Actual and Reassigned Positions

By assigning more supervisors to rank 1 all positions above rank 1 can be reduced and the top rank lowered from $R = 10$ to $R = 7$.

8.4   Flexible or Rigid Department Lines

Consider an organization with three departments $i = 1,2,3$ and work forces (operatives) $Q_1 = 11$, $Q_2 = 17$, $Q_3 = 33$. If the span of control is 3, this requires management M_i of size $M_2 = 5$, $M_2 = 8$, $M_3 = 16$. In addition, there must be a president at the top yielding a total management force of 30 persons. We will show that the number of ranks is higher under the present division of the labor and management force than is required by the aggregate system. Assigning supervisors to the lowest possible ranks yields:

	1	2	3	$\sum$	Total Organization
n_0	11	17	33	61	61
n_1	3	5	11	19	20
n_2	1	2	3	6	7
n_3	1	1	1	3	2
			1	1	1
				1	

Table 8.4.   Assigned Positions

Under the department system the president would have a rank of 5.
The combined organization can be split into three parts also, of
which two are headed by a manager of rank 3 and one by a manager of
rank 2. A rank 2 manager can head a department with 9 operatives
or less, a manager of rank 3 a department with 27 operatives or
less. A rearrangement of department sizes such that

$$Q_1 = 9, \quad Q_2 = 25, \quad Q_3 = 27$$

while not saving total personnel would allow supervising the task
with lower ranking managers and with a president of rank 4 rather
than rank 5. The total rank sums $\sum_{r=0}^{R} rn_r$ are

before	49
after	44
saving	5

<u>Problem</u>: Draw the organization charts under the old and the
proposed new department structure.

8.5 Leanness of Organizations

Organizations may be compared and partially ordered also when
ranks are not minimized. As a measure of leanness we propose
N_r, the number of positions in rank r and higher.

<u>Definition</u>: An organizational design 1 is leaner than an
organizational design 2 if, for the same size of task Q

$$N_r^1 \leqslant N_r^2 \quad \text{for all} \quad r = 0, 1, \ldots$$

and

$$N_r^1 < N_r^2 \quad \text{for some} \quad r.$$

(1)

(1) defines a partial ordering among organizations with the same task size by their leanness.

Observe that $N_0^1 < N_0^2$ implies that organization 2 has more than the minimal number $\{\frac{sQ-1}{s-1}\}$ of organization members required for task Q. Also

$$N_R^1 < N_R^2 = 1$$

implies that $N_R^1 = 0$ so that organization 1 has a lower top rank than organization 2.

<u>Definition</u>: An organizational design is efficient if, for given Q, N_r is minimal at all levels $r = 0, 1, \ldots, R, R+1, \ldots$
The following theorem presents a simple test of efficiency.

<u>Theorem</u>: Necessary and sufficient for an organizational design to be efficient is that

$$N_{r+1} = \{\frac{N_r - 1}{s}\} \tag{2}$$

<u>Proof</u>: We know from (7.2.3) that

$$N_{r+1} \geq \{\frac{N_r - 1}{s}\}$$

Recall that ranks $r+1$ and higher contain all the supervisions of personnel in ranks r or higher. Thus

$$N_{r+1} \geq \frac{1}{s} (N_r - 1).$$

Moreover, N_{r+1} must be integer. It remains to be shown that the = can be taken on for all $r = 0, \ldots, R-1$. This is in fact the case for assignments resulting from the algorithm for a rank-minimizing assignment (Section 8.3). To see this, recall that under this assignment (cf. (8.3.4), (8.3.5)

$$n_{r+1} = [\frac{n_r + o_r}{s}] \qquad o_{r+1} = n_r + o_r - s \cdot n_{r+1} \tag{3}$$

<u>Lemma 1</u>: $s \mid N_r + o_r - 1$ provided $s-1 \mid Q-1$.

<u>Proof</u> (induction): This is true for $r = 0$ because $o_0 = 0$ and $s \mid N-1$ since

$$N = \frac{sQ-1}{s-1} \qquad N-1 = \frac{sQ-s}{s-1} = s \frac{Q-1}{s-1}$$

Suppose it is true for r. Consider

$$N_{r+1} + o_{r+1} - 1 = N_r - n_r + n_r + o_r - sn_{r+1} - 1$$

using the definition of N_{r+1} and (3)

$$= N_r + o_r - 1 + - sn_{r+1}$$

$$= k \cdot s - s \cdot n_{r+1}$$

using the induction hypothesis. $\|$

<u>Corollary</u>: Under the rank-minimizing assignment rule and if $s-1 \mid Q-1$

$$N_{r+1} = \frac{N_r + o_r - 1}{s} \qquad \text{is integer.}$$

<u>Lemma 2</u>: Under the rank-minimizing assignment rule

$$N_{r+1} = \{\frac{N_r - 1}{s}\}$$

Proof: Assume first that $s-1 | Q-1$. Then

$$N_{r+1} = \frac{N_r + o_r - 1}{s} \qquad \text{is integer by the Corollary.}$$

From $0 \leqslant o_r < s$ it follows that

$$N_{r+1} = \frac{N_r - 1}{s}$$

When $s-1 | Q-1$ $\quad N_1 = \{\frac{N_0 - 1}{1}\}$. The rest of the argument is unchanged. $||$

When $s-1 | Q-1$ then the rank minimizing algorithm requires raising Q to Q^1 until $s-1 | Q^1-1$. Equivalently this means raising $N - N_0$ to N^1 until $s | N^1-1$. Therefore

$$N_1 = M = \frac{N^1 - 1}{s} = \frac{N-1}{s} = \frac{N_0 - 1}{s}.$$

For $r > 1$ the proof is the same as when $s-1 | Q-1$.

8.6 Support Structure

Some organizations are much larger than the size of the task plus required supervision mandates. This can be due to the presence of a support structure.

We consider an organization, like the Army, which contains support staff supplying necessary services to both supervisors and operatives.

Let each person in the organization require the services of $\frac{1}{m}$ support persons. As before let

Q = number of operatives
M = number of supervisors
B = number of support personnel
N = size of the organization.

By hypothesis

$$M = \frac{1}{s} (Q + M+B-1) \qquad (1)$$

$$B = \frac{1}{m} (Q+M+B) \qquad (2)$$

A straightforward calculation yields

$$B = \frac{Q+M}{m-1}$$

$$N = Q+M+B = \frac{Q+M}{1 - \frac{1}{m}}$$

$$M = \frac{1}{s} (N-1) = \frac{1}{s} \left(\frac{Q+M}{1 - \frac{1}{m}} - 1 \right)$$

$$M = \frac{m(Q-1) + 1}{(s-1)(m-1) - 1} \qquad (3)$$

$$B = \frac{sQ-1}{(s-1)(m-1) - 1} \qquad (4)$$

$$N = \frac{sQ-1}{s(1 - \frac{1}{m}) - 1} \qquad (5)$$

As an illustration suppose that

$$s = 3 \quad m = 2. \quad \text{Then}$$

$$M = 2Q-1$$

$$B = 3Q-1$$

$$N = 6Q-2.$$

The combination of support and supervision can thus blow up the size of an organization considerably.

<u>Problems</u>

1.   Let s_r be the (average) span of control for supervisors of rank r.   Show that counting up in the assignment of rank implies

$$\frac{n_{r-1}}{n_r} \leqq s_r$$

and that counting down implies

$$\frac{n_{r-1}}{n_r} = s_r .$$

2.   Suppose that the span of control for supervising supervisors is s   and for supervising operatives is s_1. Show that the amount of supervision generated by Q operatives is

$$M = \frac{sQ - s_1}{(s-1)s_1}$$

and the size of the organization required is

$$N = \frac{(s + \frac{s}{s_1} - 1)Q - 1}{s-1} .$$

(Note: It is assumed that the president does no operative work.)

3.   Suppose that it is considered desirable that first line supervisors also do some operative work and that managers, in general, do some (supervisory) work that is assigned to managers under their (immediate) supervision. What does this imply for

the size of the organization
the number of operatives
the number of supervisors
the number of ranks required?

4. Let s = 2 and Q = 4.

1) How large is the organization?
2) Find all organization charts.
3) Identify the balanced organizations.
4) Assign maximal and minimal ranks where different to positions in unbalanced organizations.

9 Regular Organization

9.1 <u>Construction</u>

The condition (7.2.3) developed in Chapter 7.

$$N_{r+1} \geqq \{\frac{N_r - 1}{s}\} \tag{1}$$

states how many higher ranking positions are needed to supervise
all positions down to rank r. If the organizational design is
efficient, it tells the required positions in ranks above r
<u>regardless of what the structure is below rank r.</u>
Rewrite (1)

$$N_{r+1} \geqq \frac{N_r + o_r - 1}{s}$$

$$N_r \leqq 1 + sN_{r+1} - o_r$$

$$N_r \leqq 1 + sN_{r+1} \tag{2}$$

$$\text{"="} \quad \text{iff} \quad o_r = 0.$$

Let R be given, $N_R = 1$. Repeated application of (2) yields

$$N_r \leqslant 1 + s(1+s(\ldots (1 + sN_R) \ldots))$$

$$\leqslant 1 + s + s^2 + \ldots + s^{R-r}N_R$$

In particular

$$N_0 \leqslant 1 + s + s^2 + \ldots s^R \tag{3}$$

since $N_R = 1.$

The upper bound given by (3) is achieved in a regular organization.

<u>Proposition</u>. In a regular organization

$$n_r = s^{R-r} \tag{4}$$

<u>Proof</u>: Summation of (4) yields (3).

A regular organization is thus a balanced organization with constant span of control. In particular, an organization is called regular when all its operatives have rank zero and all supervisors have a constant span of control s.

9.2 Properties

An organization of this type has an ideal structure which may be characterized as follows. It has no slack and makes maximal use of the capacity to supervise: No person of rank $r > 0$ performs operative work. Therefore:

   i) For a given s and R the size of the task Q is maximized.
   ii) For a given s and Q the maximal rank R is minimized.
   iii) For a given Q and R the maximal span of control s is minimized.

To prove property i) observe that

$$Q = \frac{1}{s} + \frac{s-1}{s} N$$

is a linear function of N and is maximized when N is. From (3) it follows that a regular organization maximizes $N_0 - N$. ||

Properties (ii) and (iii) are corollaries.
Mathematically, the regular organization is characterized by (4).
The image of a regular organization as a pyramid is, therefore,
misleading. The basis is much broader, since the number of
positions increases exponentially as one moves down the hierarchy
of ranks.

The number of persons of rank r or higher rank is

$$N_r = 1 + s + \ldots + s^{R-r} = \frac{s^{R-r+1} - 1}{s-1} \tag{5}$$

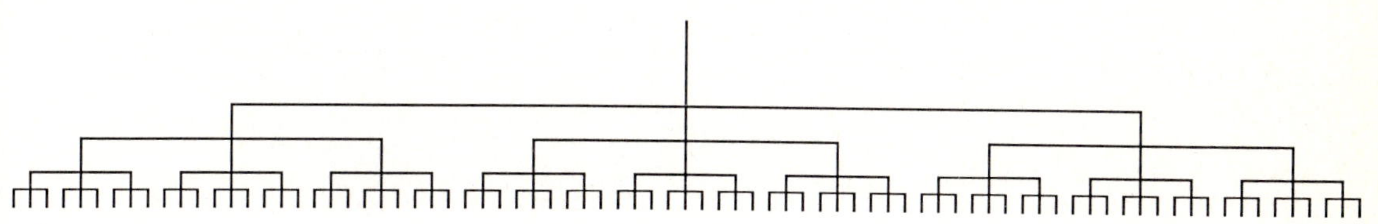

Figure 9.1. Regular Organization with $s = 3$, $R = 4$

9.3 Average Rank

Average rank is defined as

$$\bar{r} = \frac{\sum\limits_{r=0}^{R} rn_r}{n_r} = \frac{1}{s-1} - \frac{R+1}{s^{R+1} - 1} \tag{6}$$

Average rank increases with maximal rank R, but remains bounded and approaches rapidly this bound

$$\overline{r} \leqq \frac{1}{s-1} \leqq 1 \quad \text{for} \quad s > 1 \tag{7}$$

This bound $\frac{1}{s-1}$ is itself not larger than unity when the span of control is at least 2.

Notice that the fraction

$$\frac{s^{R}(s-1)}{s^{R+1} - 1} = 1 - \frac{1}{s}$$

of all members of a regular organization have rank zero.

<u>Proposition.</u> The average rank in a regular organization is minimal among all organizations with given Q and s.

This is a special case of the proposition that cost of a given output is minimized by a regular organization (see Section 10.3).

9.4 Average Distance

Consider next the average distance between the president and all members of the organization.

$$\overline{d}_{R} = R - \overline{r}$$

Substituting for $\overline{r}$

$$\overline{d}_{R} = R - \frac{1}{s-1} + \frac{R+1}{s^{R+1} - 1} \tag{8}$$

The average distance from the president in an organization is minimal among all organizations of given s and Q. The reason for this is that R is minimal while $\frac{1}{s-1}$ is small and

$$\frac{R+1}{s^{R+1}-1}$$ is negligible.

However, in the set of all balanced organizations, the regular organization has a maximal average distance between president and organization members. The reason is that the number of organization members at large distances is maximized. In fact, it is maximal, and not minimal, for a regular organization among all balanced organizations of radius R. Moreover, with a given bound on this span of control, average distance from the president in a regular organization is maximal among all organizations of given s and given diameter (maximal distance between members) D.

The most interesting properties of regular organizations relate to the fact that unit costs are minimal. These are developed in section 10.5 below.

<u>Problem</u>: Derive n_r and N_r when

$$s_R = s-1 \quad s_r = s \quad r = 1, 2, \ldots, R-1.$$

Notice that the expression for N_r is simpler than (5).

10 Costs

10.1 <u>Salary Schedules</u>

Small organizations can set salaries on an individual
basis. Large organizations require a general schema. The
principal variables determining salaries are

> rank and
>
> length of service.

Presumably, these are intended to capture the principal
components of managerial performance: ability as demonstrated by
past performance reflected in rank and knowledge of the
organization's procedures as reflected in length of service.

Typically rank determines a salary range, and length of
service a point in this range.

In principle, salaries may be any increasing function of
rank and any nondecreasing function of length of service. It is
typically a sum or product of a function of rank and of a
function of service. In addition, there may be other factors
measuring merit apart from rank, i.e., performance in this rank
so far.

A reasonable requirement concerning the relationship between
rank and salary is the following: each increase in rank by one
unit should generate an increase of utility by one unit (or by a
constant amount). This translates the relationship between rank
and salary into one between utility and money.

The following types of cardinal utility functions have been
used in mathematical economics and econometrics. (They are all
subject to linear transformations.)

<u>linear utility</u> $u(w) = w$

<u>logarithmic utility</u> $u(w) = \ln w$

<u>constant elasticity</u> $u(w) = \begin{cases} w^\lambda & 0 < \lambda \leqslant 1 \\ -w^{-\lambda} & \lambda < 0 \end{cases}$

To obtain a salary schedule with unit increments of utility from a utility function write the inverse function ϕ

$$w = \phi(u)$$

and let

$$u = r$$

i.e., after a linear transformation utility is equal to rank r. Thus

$$w_r = \phi(r).$$

The above examples give rise to

<u>linear salary schedule</u>
$$w_r = w_0 + ar$$

<u>exponential salary schedule</u> $\quad w_r = e^{\alpha_0 + \alpha r}$
$$w_r = w_0 a^r$$
where $\quad a = e^\alpha$

<u>power scale</u> $\qquad w_r = \alpha_0 + \alpha \cdot r^{\left|\frac{1}{\lambda}\right|}$
$$= w_0 (1+ar)^b$$

with $\quad a = \dfrac{\alpha}{\alpha_0}$

$$b = \left|\frac{1}{\lambda}\right|$$

In practice, pure systems are rare and compromises prevail. These may be the results of a number of uniform and proportionate salary increases in the past.

Certain properties are valid for all salary functions that are monotone increasing. Calculation of average cost and average wages requires, however, a specification of the salary schedule.

While organizations can create certain positions and set the associated salaries at will, the salary structure for supervisory positions in organizations is not arbitrary, and cannot be understood simply from utility considerations. In Chapter 19 it will be shown how the opportunity costs for managers in organizations are determined. They are the profits that the heads of organizations of similar size could earn, and these profits are in turn derived from the advantage of organizations of various size.

10.2 Average Wage and Unit Labor Cost

So far the input into an organization was considered in terms of persons only. As soon as money cost is considered, one must recognize the fact that personnel cost depends on personnel rank. Setting aside for the moment problems of motivation and qualification, economy of labor cost is economy of rank. An arrangement that minimizes rank for each person also minimizes labor cost. In the following only labor costs are considered. This is justified when the wage bill dominates all other costs or when other costs are a well-defined monotone increasing function of personnel cost such as when total cost is proportional to labor cost. For simplicity we shall describe personnel cost as wages. This must be taken to include all forms of compensation and the money equivalent of other perquisites and fringe benefits as well.

In any organization without slack there is a simple relationship between average wage and unit labor cost.

We assume that wages depend only on rank, $w = w_r$.

$$\text{Let} \qquad W = \sum_{r=0}^{R} n_r w_r \qquad (1)$$

be the total wage bill. Then unit labor cost is

$$\bar{c} = \frac{W}{Q}. \qquad (2)$$

and average wage is

$$\bar{w} = \frac{W}{N}. \qquad (3)$$

In Chapter 6, it was shown that in organizations without slack

$$N = \frac{sQ-1}{s-1} \qquad \text{or} \qquad (4)$$

$$Q = \frac{1+(s-1)N}{s} \qquad (5)$$

Therefore,

$$\bar{w} = \frac{W}{N} = \frac{W(s-1)}{Qs-1} = \frac{\bar{c} \cdot (s-1)}{s - \frac{1}{Q}} \qquad (6)$$

$$\bar{c} = \frac{W}{Q} = \frac{W \cdot s}{1+(s-1)N} = \frac{\bar{w} \cdot s}{s-1 + \frac{1}{N}} \qquad (7)$$

Equation (6) and (7) state the relationship between average wage and unit labor cost. For large organizations $N \gg 1$ or $Q \gg 1$ one has approximately

$$\bar{c} \approx \frac{\bar{w}}{1 - \frac{1}{s}} \qquad (8)$$

Thus unit labor cost is approximately

$$\frac{1}{1 - \frac{1}{s}}$$ times average wage.

This relationship holds regardless of the ranks of

operatives. The factor $\frac{1}{1 - \frac{1}{s}}$ was introduced in Chapter 4 as

the organizational multiplier. It is now revealed as the ratio of unit cost to average wage.

10.3 Cost Minimizing Organizational Designs

Let the size of the task be given, either in terms of Q, or of operative workloads q_r for various ranks r. We also assume that hiring is for full-time positions and the organizational design satisfies the efficiency criterion of 8.5

$$N_{r+1} \geq \{\frac{N_r - 1}{s}\} \tag{9}$$

In the case that operative work is done at higher levels write

$$Q_r = \sum_{i=1}^{R} q_i$$

The condition (9) must then be restated in terms of managerial personnel m_r at levels r and of

$$M_r = \sum_{i=1}^{R} m_i$$

as follows

$$M_{r+1} \geq \{\frac{M_r + Q_r - 1}{s}\} \tag{9'}$$

(9) or (9') state the minimal personnel requirements that are created by the given workload Q_r.

Subject to (9) or (9') we seek to minimize total labor cost $\sum_{r=0}^{R} w_r n_r$. Restating this in terms of N_r or M_r and Q_r and letting $N_{R+1} = 0$, $M_{R+1} = 0$, $Q_{R+1} = 0$ the problem is

$$\operatorname*{Min}_{N_r} \sum_{r=0}^{R} w_r (N_r - N_{r+1}) \tag{10}$$

subject to (9)

or

$$\operatorname*{Min}_{M_r} \sum_{r=0}^{R} w_r (M_r - M_{r+1} + Q_r - Q_{r+1}) \tag{10'}$$

subject to (9')

Recall that Q_r is given.

The sum (10) may be rewritten

$$\sum_{r=0}^{R} w_r (N_r - N_{r+1}) = w_0 N_0 + \sum_{r=1}^{R} N_r (w_r - w_{r-1}) \tag{11}$$

Observe now that $w_0 > 0$ and that w_r increases with r so that all coefficients of N_r $r = 0, \ldots, R$ in (14) are positive. Hence, minimizing total cost is achieved by minimizing every N_r. Necessary and sufficient for this is that the "=" sign applies in every constraint (9).

In the same way it follows that the "=" sign must apply in all inequalities (9'). Thus

<u>Theorem:</u> An organizational design for a given task is cost minimizing if and only if it is efficient.

Notice that the cost minimizing design is independent of the salary schedule, as long as $w_{r+1} > w_r$ holds for all r.

10.4 <u>Job Allocation in the Short Run</u>

Suppose the organizational structure N_r is given and that a particular job of size $q \leqslant 1$ is to be performed. The opportunity cost of using one person unit at level r is w_r and there are no capacity constraints. Let job q be done in amounts x_r at levels r and let x_{ir} $i > r$ denote the necessary supervision of persons in rank r by persons in rank i. The constraints are

$$\sum_{r=0}^{R} x_r \geq q \tag{1}$$

$$s \sum_{i=r+1}^{R} x_{ir} \geq \sum_{j=0}^{r-1} s_{rj} + x_r \tag{2}$$

Subject to constraints (1) and (2) we seek to

$$\mathop{\text{Min}}_{\substack{x_r \geq 0 \\ x_{rj} \geq 0}} \sum_{r=0}^{R} w_r (x_r + \sum_{j=0}^{r-1} x_{rj}) \tag{3}$$

Under the stated conditions this program is feasible. The efficiency conditions for this linear program are as follows. Let μ be the efficiency price (dual variable) for constraint (1), λ_r the dual variables for constraints (2), $r = 1, \ldots, R$. Then

$$x_r \begin{Bmatrix} = \\ \geq \end{Bmatrix} 0 \quad <=> \quad \mu \begin{Bmatrix} < \\ = \end{Bmatrix} w_r + \lambda_r$$

or

$$\mu = \underset{r}{\text{Min}} \; (w_r + \lambda_r)$$

$$x_{ij} \left\{ \begin{matrix} = \\ \geq \end{matrix} \right\} \; 0 \quad <=> \quad s\lambda_j \left\{ \begin{matrix} \leq \\ = \end{matrix} \right\} \; w_i + \lambda_i \qquad i > j$$

or

$$\lambda_r = \frac{1}{s} \; \underset{i>r}{\text{Min}} \; (w_i + \lambda_i)$$

The following results can be shown. Let $w_r = w_0 a^r$.

<u>Proposition</u>

Provided $R > R^*$ is sufficiently large, then

$$x_0 = q, \quad x_r = 0 \quad \text{for all} \quad r > 0$$

$$\mu = w_0 \frac{1 - (\frac{a}{s})^{R+1}}{1 - \frac{a}{s}}$$

$$x_{r,r-1} = qs^{-r} \qquad r = 1, \ldots, R$$

$$\lambda_r = \frac{1}{s-a} [a^{r+1} - s^{r+1}(\frac{a}{s})^{R+1}] \qquad r = 1, \ldots, R-1$$

$$\lambda_R = 0$$

In words, the optimal assignment of jobs is to operatives in rank
zero. The cheapest method of supervision is to extend a full
chain of supervisors through ranks r to R.

Only for organizations of lower height R can it happen
that direct supervision by the president is the cheapest
solution. (This is always true in a simple organization.)

μ is the least cost of performing a job of unit size; λ_r is the least cost of supervising one unit of work in rank r.

10.5 Minimizing Unit Labor Cost

So far the size of the task was assumed given. Suppose, however, that the organization can choose the task size to minimize average costs.

To illustrate this problem, consider all organizations using integer numbers of supervisors and operatives when $s = 3$ and $Q = 1, \ldots, 9$ (Table 10.1). Clearly unit labor cost is locally minimal for $Q = 1,3$ and 9, all representing regular organizations. However, there is also a minimum at $Q = 5$.

$Q = n_0$	1	2	3	4	5	6
n_1	0	1	1	2	3	2
n_2	0	0	0	1	1	1
C	w_0	$w_1 + 2w_0$	$w_1 + 3w_0$	$4w_0 + 2w_1 + w_2$	$5w_0 + 2w_1 + w_2$	$6w_0 + 2w_1 + w_2$
$\bar{c}$	w_0	$w_0 + \dfrac{w_1}{2}$	$w_0 + \dfrac{w_1}{3}$	$w_0 + \dfrac{w_1}{2} + \dfrac{w_2}{4}$	$w_0 + \dfrac{2}{5} w_1 + w_2$	$w_0 + \dfrac{1}{3} w_1 + \dfrac{w_2}{6}$

$Q = n_0$	7	8	9	10
n_1	3	3	3	3
n_2	1	1	1	1
C	$7w_0 + 3w_1 + w_2$	$8w_0 + 3w_1 + w_2$	$9w_0 + 3w_1 + w_2$	$10w_0 + 3w_1 + w_2 + w_3$
$\bar{c}$	$w_0 + \dfrac{3}{7} w_1 + \dfrac{w_2}{7}$	$w_0 + \dfrac{3}{8} w_1 + \dfrac{w_2}{8}$	$w_0 + \dfrac{1}{3} w_1 + \dfrac{w_2}{9}$	$w_0 + \dfrac{3}{10} w_1 + \dfrac{w_2}{10} + \dfrac{w_3}{10}$

Table 10.1. Comparison of Unit Labor Costs

To compare average cost for regular and nonregular organizations denote the size of a regular organization with R supervisory levels by $N(R)$ and consider the ratios N_r/N in the range $N(R) \leqslant N \leqslant N(R+1)$.

<u>Lemma 1</u>: For efficient organizations with N in the range

$$N(R) \leqslant N \leqslant N(R+1) \tag{1}$$

one has

$$\frac{N_R}{N} \geqq \frac{1}{s^r} - \frac{1}{N} \sum_{i=1}^{r} s^{-i} \qquad r = 0, \ldots, R+1 \tag{2}$$

and $"="$ only for $N = N(R)$.

<u>Proof</u>: $\quad N_{r+1} = \dfrac{N_r - 1 + o_r}{s} \qquad 0 \leqslant o_r < s \quad$ from (8.5.2).

Successive substitution yields

$$N_r = \frac{1}{s}\,(-1 + o_{r-1} + \frac{1}{s}\,(-1 + o_{r-2} + \frac{1}{s}\,(\ldots)$$

$$= \sum_{i=1}^{r} \frac{o_i - 1}{s^i} + \frac{1}{s^r}\,N_0 .$$

From this, using $N_0 = N$

$$\frac{N_r}{N} = \frac{1}{s^r} + \frac{1}{N} \sum_{i=1}^{r} \frac{o_i - 1}{s^i}$$

$$\geqq \frac{1}{s^r} - \frac{1}{N} \sum_{i=1}^{r} \frac{1}{s^i}$$

$$\frac{N_r}{N} \geqq \frac{1}{s^r} - \frac{1}{N}\,\frac{1 - s^{-r}}{s - 1} \tag{2a}$$

The "=" applies if and only if all $o_r = 0$, i.e., for a regular organization. $\|$

Corollary 2:
$$\underset{N(R) \leqslant N \leqslant N(R+1)}{\text{Min}} \frac{N_r}{N} = \frac{s^{R-r+1} - 1}{s^{R+1} - 1} \tag{3}$$

Proof: The right-hand side in (3) is a decreasing function of N, and the "=" applies when $N = N(R)$. Substituting

$$N(R) = \frac{s^{R+1} - 1}{s-1} \quad \text{yields the assertion.} \ \|$$

Lemma 3: In the range

$$N(R) \leqslant N \leqslant N(R+1) \tag{1}$$

average wage

$$\overline{w} = \frac{C(N)}{N}$$

is minimized for $N = N(R)$, i.e., for a regular organization.

Proof: Recall from (10.3.11) that

$$C = C(N) = w_0 N + \sum_{r=1}^{R} (w_r - w_{r-1}) N_r \tag{4}$$

Hence $\overline{w} = \dfrac{C}{N} = w_0 + \displaystyle\sum_{r=1}^{R} (w_r - w_{r-1}) \dfrac{N_r}{N}$

The assertion follows from Corollary 2. $\|$

A regular organization has not only minimal cost for its given output but also minimum average cost among all organizations of size $N(R)$ or larger. This is the content of

<u>Theorem 4</u>:   Let $N(R)$ be the size of a regular organization.
Then

$$\overline{w}(N) = \frac{C(N)}{N} > \frac{C(N(R))}{N(R)} \quad \text{for all} \quad N > N(R).$$

<u>Proof</u>:   For $N(R) < N \leqslant N(R+1)$ this is the statement of Lemma 3.
For $N \geqslant N(R+1)$ it follows successively from Lemma 3 and the
observation that

$$\overline{w}(R+1) = \frac{C(N(R+1))}{N(R+1)} = w_0 + \sum_{r=1}^{R+1} (w_r - w_{r-1}) \frac{N_r}{N}$$

$$> w_0 + \sum_{r=1}^{R} (w_r - w_{r-1}) \frac{N_r}{N}$$

$$> \overline{w}(R)$$

by Lemma 3. ||

This proof shows that average wage (or unit cost) in regular
organizations increase with the number of levels R.

10.6   <u>Costs and Scale for Regular Organization</u>

To study how average cost in a regular organization increases
with R one must specify w_r.   Let salaries follow an exponential
schedule

$$w_r = w_0 g^r \tag{5}$$

<u>Lemma 5</u>:   For a regular organization with salary scheme (5)
average wage is

$$\overline{w}(R) = w_0 \cdot \frac{1 - \frac{1}{s}}{1 - \frac{g}{s}} \cdot \frac{1 - (\frac{g}{s})^{R+1}}{1 = (\frac{1}{s})^{R+1}} \tag{6}$$

Proof:
$$\overline{w} = w_0 \frac{\sum n_r g^r}{N} = w \cdot \sum_{r=0}^{R} \left(\frac{g}{s}\right)^r$$

$$= \frac{w_0 \sum_{r=0}^{R} s^{R-r} g^r (s-1)}{s^{R+1} - 1}$$

or

$$\overline{w}(R) = w_0 \frac{1 - \frac{1}{s}}{1 - \frac{g}{s}} \frac{1 - \left(\frac{g}{s}\right)^{R+1}}{1 - \left(\frac{1}{s}\right)^{R+1}} \qquad ||$$

Observe that since $g > 1$ this is an increasing function of R. But it approaches rapidly the limiting value

$$\lim_{R \to \infty} \overline{w}(R) = w_0 \frac{1 - \frac{1}{s}}{1 - \frac{g}{s}} \qquad \text{for} \quad 0 < \delta < s \qquad (7)$$

Lemma 6: In a regular organization the average wage $\overline{w}$ is asymptotically constant and equal to

$$w_0 \frac{1 - \frac{1}{s}}{1 - \frac{g}{s}} \qquad (7)$$

Example: Let $s = 4$, $g = \frac{4}{3}$

$$\overline{w} = w_0 \frac{1 - \frac{1}{4}}{1 - \frac{1}{3}} = \frac{9}{8} = 1.125$$

Corollary 7: If R is sufficiently large, the average cost $\frac{C}{Q}$ for a regular organization of size $N(R)$ is smaller than that for any other organization of size $N \geqslant N(R)$ with the same salary structure and span of control.

Proof: For sufficiently large R, equation (10.2.11) says that

$$\overline{c} = \frac{C}{Q} \approx \frac{1}{1 - \frac{1}{s}} \overline{w} \qquad ||$$

<u>Lemma 8</u>:   In a regular organization of R supervisory levels average cost equals

$$\bar{c} = \frac{w_0}{1 - \frac{g}{s}} \cdot [1 - (\frac{g}{s})^{R+1}] \tag{8}$$

It increases with R and approaches rapidly the limit

$$\bar{c} \doteq \frac{w_0}{1 - \frac{g}{s}} \tag{9}$$

<u>Proof</u>:

$$\bar{c} = \frac{C}{Q} = \frac{w_0 \sum\limits_{r=0}^{R} s^{R-r} g^r}{s^R}$$

$$= w_0 \sum\limits_{r=0}^{R} (\frac{g}{s})^r$$

$$= w_0 \frac{1 - (\frac{g}{s})^{R+1}}{1 - \frac{g}{s}}$$

by the well-known summation formula for the geometric series. $\|$ For small R average costs may be minimal when the organization is non-regular as shown by the following example.

$$s = 3, \ Q = 5, \quad \bar{C} = w_0 + \frac{w_1}{5} + \frac{w_2}{5}$$

$$s = 3, \ Q = 9 \text{ (regular)}, \quad \bar{C} = w_0 + \frac{1}{3} w_1 + \frac{1}{9} w_2$$

But

$$\bar{C}(9) \leqslant \bar{C}(5) \quad \text{only when} \quad \frac{w_1}{3} + \frac{w_2}{9} \leqslant \frac{w_1}{5} + \frac{w_2}{5}$$

$$\text{or} \quad w_2 \geqslant \frac{3}{2} w_1$$

which, incidentally, is unlikely to be true in practice.

10.7 Cost and Scale for Nonregular Organizations

In a regular organization average wage and unit costs are strictly bounded. Consider, however, a simple type of nonregular organization, described by Figure 10.1, an s-ladder:

$$n_R = 1$$

$$n_r = s \qquad r = 0,1, \ldots, R-1$$

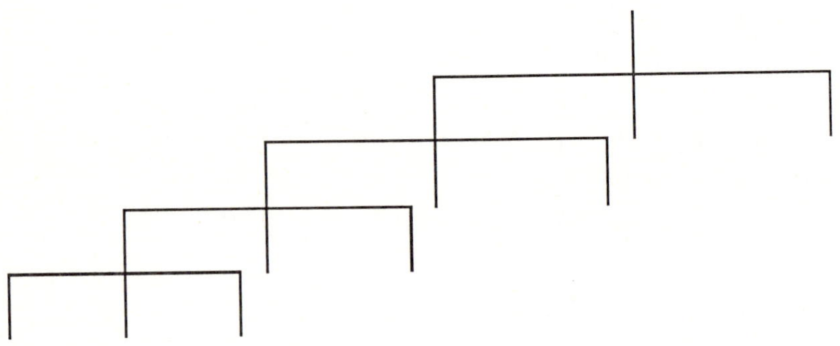

Figure 10.1.   s-ladder

There is only one supervisory position at every level. The number of operatives is

$$Q = s + (R-1)(s-1) = 1 + R \cdot (s-1) \qquad (1)$$

the total number of positions is

$$N = 1 + sR$$

and the wage bill is

$$C = w_R + s(w_{R-1} + w_{R-2} + \cdots + w_1 + w_0) \qquad (2)$$

Therefore, average wages are

$$\overline{w} = \frac{w_R + s(w_{R-1} + \cdots + w_0)}{1 + sR} \qquad (3)$$

and unit labor costs are

$$\overline{c} = \frac{w_R + s(w_{R-1} + \cdots + w_0)}{1 + (s-1)R} \qquad (4)$$

Consider the unweighted mean wage

$$\overline{w}_R = \frac{w_0 + w_1 + \cdots + w_R}{R + 1} \qquad (5)$$

In terms of this the average wage (3) may be written

$$\overline{w} = \frac{w_R + sR\overline{w}_{R-1}}{1 + sR} \qquad (6)$$

$$> \overline{w}_{R-1}$$

provided

$$w_R > w_{R-1} > \cdots > w_1 > w_0. \qquad (7)$$

If the wage sequence w_r is unbounded, it follows that average wage in an organization of the s-ladder type increases without bound.

Similarly consider unit labor cost

$$\bar{c} = \frac{w_R + sR\bar{w}_{R-1}}{1 + (s-1)R}$$

$$> \frac{s}{s-1}\ \bar{w}_{R-1}$$

provided (7) applies. Once more unit labor cost increases without bound when wages w_r increase without bound.

Specifically when

$$w_r = g^r \tag{8}$$

the unweighted mean wage is

$$\bar{w}_{R-1} = \frac{1 + g + \ldots + g^{R-1}}{R} = \frac{g^R - 1}{R(g-1)} \tag{9}$$

and since $g > 1$ this lower bound increases with R without limits. We conclude that in nonregular organizations average wage and unit cost may increase without limit as the organization's height R is increased.

Problem

Let every manager (line supervisor) have a staff headed by a staff person whose rank is one below the manager's. Let the span of control for staff be $\sigma \leq s$ where s is the uniform line span of control. Show that in a regular line organization with staff unit costs are bounded and asymptotically constant provided $\sigma < s$. Calculate unit costs as a function of R when $\sigma = s$.

III Productivity and Structure

So far, output Q was measured in units of input of operative labor L.

$$Q = \phi L \qquad \phi \equiv 1 \tag{1}$$

This assumes that labor productivity ϕ is constant. What if productivity ϕ depends on organizational structure?

We consider three possible scenarios

$\phi = \phi(R)$ productivity depends on the height of the organization, the number of hierarchical levels

$\phi = \phi(N)$ productivity depends on size

This is the classical issue of increasing, constant or decreasing returns to scale. We are not concerned here with scale economies in production, rather with those of administration or management. This must depend directly on R and s and only indirectly on N since $N = s^R$.

$\phi = \phi(s)$

To study this we shall examine simple organizations, those with only one manager. In that case

$$N = s+1.$$

We begin with the study of $\phi = \phi(s)$ and consider how productivity is affected in simple organizations by

substitutability of operative and management inputs (ch. 11)

cost of information (ch. 12) and

loss of information (ch. 13).

After that we examine $\phi = \phi(s)$ in multi-level organizations by considering

loss of information and

unchecked loss of control (ch. 14).

Some uses of production functions are described in chs. 15 and 16. Rather than considering these issues in the abstract we shall analyze them in terms of illustrative examples.

11 Substitution of Management and Operative Inputs: Welfare Agency*

In this section we consider a simple organization whose output may be measured in terms of "cases handled". The analysis uses elementary queuing theory. In view of the restrictiveness of this queuing model, the results should be considered as illustrative rather than definitive.

Examples of organization tasks that can be described as cases are:

law suits,

auditing of income tax returns,

adjusting insurance claims,

determining and monitoring the eligibility of welfare applicants.

There are, of course, many other intances where paper work can be divided into simple units to be labelled cases.

11.1 A Queuing Model

To begin with we consider a simple organization consisting of $x_1 = 1$ supervisor and x_0 caseworkers. Each case worker has a well-defined area of competence, determined by either geographical or technical criteria that are easy to verify. Cases arrive at random, and are assigned without delay to the appropriate caseworker by the supervisor's office. The areas of competence are delimited in such a way that each caseworker receives on the average the same case load per period. If cases arrive at random at a rate λ, then those assigned to a particular caseworker arrive at random at a rate λ.

*This chapter is based on Beckmann, 1982.

Define the completion rate at which a caseworker handles cases to be μ_0 and assume this to be the same for each caseworker. Alternatively we may say that the average time needed by a caseworker to complete a case is $\frac{1}{\mu_0}$.

Introduce now the rather special assumption that the completion times are exponentially distributed with mean $\frac{1}{\mu_0}$. (This is relaxed in Section 11.4 below.) Then it is well-known that cases will spend an average length of time

$$\frac{1}{\mu_0 - \frac{\lambda}{x_0}} \tag{1}$$

with the respective caseworker [Wagner, 1969]. When a caseworker has finished a case, it is then passed back to the supervisor for possible inspection, verification, and signing. The supervisors' completion rate is defined to be μ_1, that is, the average time required for inspection, verification, and signing is $\frac{1}{\mu_1}$. Once more assume that this time is exponentially distributed with mean $\frac{1}{\mu_1}$. A case will then spend an average time

$$\frac{1}{\mu_1 - \frac{\lambda}{x_1}} \tag{2}$$

while waiting for and being disposed of by the supervisor.

Although we consider $x_1 = 1$, as the normal situation, the possibility of the supervisor being available only part-time ($x_1 < 1$) is included here as a possibility. For the waiting time formula to be valid, the times of availability must be randomly chosen.

Sometimes the case will be returned to the caseworker and possibly there will be some interaction during the actual casework between worker and supervisor. All this is implicit in the (exponential) probability time distributions for casework and, therefore, need not be considered here explicitly.

The expected value of the total time that a case spends in the system on the average is now the sum of expressions (1) and (2)--a special property of exponential service times distributions. We will now introduce the importance postulate that this average time must not exceed an acceptable level τ in a well-functioning organization.

In welfare agencies operating at the county level, the State of California imposes in fact a time limit on eligibility procedures as a condition for its financial support. This time limit is meant to apply in every case, but in the face of randomness, this is clearly not a realistic requirement.

Let limit τ on average time in the system be effective

$$\frac{1}{\mu_0 - \frac{\lambda}{x_0}} + \frac{1}{\mu_1 - \frac{\lambda}{x_1}} = \tau. \tag{3}$$

Consider the system in steady-state equilibrium. The rate of case inflow λ is then also the rate of case outflow and this may be considered a measure of the output of the organization. The inputs are $x_0 = 1$ supervisor and x_0 caseworkers.

Equation (3) is an implicit definition of a production function

$$\lambda = \lambda(x_0, x_1) \tag{4}$$

in which output λ depends on two factors of production, labor x_0 and supervision x_1.

11.2 Analysis

We solve (11.1.3) in closed form and establish that it has the usual properties of a microeconomic production function.

Straightforward arithmetic yields the following quadratic equation in λ

$$\lambda^2 - 2[ax_0 + bx_1]\lambda + [4ab - \frac{1}{\tau^2}]x_0 x_1 = 0$$

where

$$2a = \mu_0 - \frac{1}{\tau} > 0$$

$$2b = \mu_1 - \frac{1}{\tau} > 0.$$

That a and b are positive is seen as follows. Notice that τ is feasible only if exceeds the requirements $\frac{1}{\mu_0}$ and $\frac{1}{\mu_1}$ at each stage for processing

$$\tau > \frac{1}{\mu_i} \qquad i = 0,1.$$

This equation is solved by

$$\lambda = ax_0 - bx_1 - \sqrt{(ax_0 - bx_1) + \frac{x_0 x_1}{\tau^2}} \, . \tag{1}$$

Notice that

$$\lambda(0, x_1) = 0$$

implies the minus sign for the square root term.

As a first property of the production function (1), we notice that output increases with τ, when x_0, x_1 are held constant. This follows by differentiation of (11.1.3)

$$\frac{\partial \tau}{\partial \lambda} = \frac{1}{(\mu_0 - \frac{\lambda}{x_0})^2 \, x_0} + \frac{1}{(\mu_1 - \frac{\lambda}{x_1})^2 \, x_1} > 0$$

τ may be considered a quality attribute of output; as τ increases quality decreases. Thus increasing quality decreases quantity of output for given inputs x_0, x_1.

That output λ is an increasing function of either input x_i is best seen from (3). The left-hand expression increases with λ and decreases with x_i so that by the implicit function theorem

$$\frac{\partial \lambda}{\partial x_i} = - \frac{\frac{\partial \tau}{\partial x_i}}{\frac{\partial \tau}{\partial \lambda}}$$

$$\text{sign} \; \frac{\partial \lambda}{\partial x_i} = - \frac{-}{+} = + \tag{2}$$

Thus the marginal product of either factor is positive. From (11.1.3) it may be shown that $\lambda(x_0, x_1)$ is linear homogeneous, but this is also apparent from (1). We introduce the ratios

$$s = \frac{x_0}{x_1}$$

$$\tag{2}$$

$$y = \frac{\lambda}{x_1}$$

Here s is the span of control and y is the output of one agency if it is headed by one full-time supervisor. Substituting s and y in (5) one has the homogenized production function in one variable

$$y = y(s) = v + as - \frac{1}{2} \sqrt{(as-b)^2 + \frac{s}{\tau^2}} \qquad (3)$$

For λ to be concave, i.e., for the law of diminishing returns to substitution to apply, it is sufficient that $y(s)$ be concave. Now a straightforward calculation shows that

$$\text{sign } y''(s) = \text{sign } (\frac{1}{\mu_0} + \frac{1}{\mu_1} - \tau)$$

$$< 0 \quad \text{if} \quad \tau \quad \text{is feasible.} \qquad (4)$$

Recall that the $\frac{1}{\mu_i}$ are the expected processing times in stage i for each case.

As a final property of the production function λ, we note that for $x_1 = 1$ (or in fact $x_1 = $ constant) the output is bounded. For letting $x_0 \to \infty$ in (11.1.3) one obtains

$$\frac{1}{\mu_0} + \frac{1}{\mu_1 - \lambda} \lneqq \tau$$

which is solved by

$$\lambda(x_0,1) < \mu_1 - \frac{1}{\tau - \frac{1}{\mu_0}}$$

for any finite x_0. Similarly for fixed x_0, the production function is bounded with respect to the variable x_1.

As an illustration consider the case with the simplest numbers

$$\mu_0 = \mu_1 = 3 \quad \tau = 1 \quad \text{satisfying (4) and implying}$$
$$a = b = 2,$$

$$\lambda = x_0 + x_1 - \sqrt{x_0^2 - x_0 x_1 + x_1^2} \tag{5}$$

By a linear transformation of the variables x_0, x_1, λ the function λ can always be standardized as (11). The homogenized version of (11)

$$y = 1 + s - \sqrt{1 - s + s^2}$$

is illustrated in Figure 11.1.

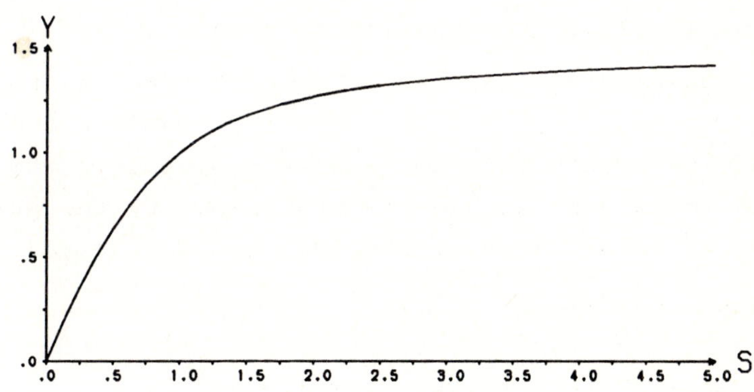

Figure 11.1

Boundedness of the production function implies that it is not well approximated by such standard types as a Cobb-Douglas function for large values of x_0, given $x_1 = 1$. Rather the production functions (11), (12) must stand on their own.

11.3 Discussion

It should be pointed out that the present model the output rate μ_0 of a caseworker does not depend on the amount of supervision $\dfrac{x_1}{x_0}$ that might be calculated to fall on one caseworker. It is not that number which is relevant, but the fact that each case goes to the supervisor for inspection and that the necessary time averaging $\frac{1}{\mu_1}$ is always applied. Thus the fact of supervision implies the necessary amount of supervision. The output rate $\frac{1}{\mu_0}$ of a caseworker is often set by general rules in an organization. Thus in welfare agencies, case load per worker is prescribed. In one California agency actual case loads for eligibility work were as follows

$$633/33 = 20.1 \quad \text{for new applications}$$

$$6,250/64 = 97.6 \quad \text{for continuing cases.}$$

Since continuing cases are to be rechecked every month, a case load of, e.g., 6,250 cases should be interpreted as a flow of 6,250 cases per month. In the budget proposal it was stated that these case loads were within the limits set by the state (these limits may be inferred as 20 and 100, respectively).

With the values

$$\mu_0 = 20 \quad \mu_1 = 100 \quad \tau = 1.5$$

one has

$$2a = 20 - \frac{1}{1.5} = 19.\overline{3}$$

$$2b = 100 - \frac{1}{1.5} = 99.\overline{3}$$

and the production function is

$$y = 49.\overline{6} + 9.\overline{6} \cdot s - \sqrt{(19.\overline{3}s - 49.\overline{6})^2 + 0.\overline{4}s} \quad (8a)$$

11.4 Generalization

In this section, we show how the assumption of exponential service time distributions can be dropped. As noted by Cox (1967)

the convergence of several streams of customers, even after being
processed with non-exponential service times, generates an
approximate Poisson stream, if the original arrivals at the
different caseworkers were independent and Poisson.

Let σ_i^2 $i = 0,1$ be the variances of the service time
distributions for caseworkers 0 and supervisors 1 respectively.
The Pollacek-Kintchin formula (Wagner 1965) states that average
delay (including service time) at station i equals

$$W_i = \frac{1}{\mu_i} + \frac{(\frac{\lambda}{x_i \mu_i})^2 + (\frac{\lambda}{x_i})^2 \sigma_i^2}{2 \frac{\lambda}{x_i} (1 - \frac{\lambda}{x_i \mu_i})}. \tag{12}$$

Adding and simplifying we obtain the total average delay τ

$$\frac{\frac{\lambda}{x_o \mu_o^2} + \frac{\lambda \sigma_o^2}{x_o}}{2(1 - \frac{\lambda}{x_o \mu_o})} + \frac{\frac{\lambda}{x_1 \mu_1^2} + \frac{\lambda \sigma_1^2}{x_1}}{2(1 - \frac{\lambda}{x_1 \mu_1})} + \frac{1}{\mu_o} + \frac{1}{\mu_1} = \tau. \tag{13}$$

Once more equation (13) defines a production function

$$\lambda = \lambda(x_o, x_1, \tau).$$

It may be found in closed form by solving the quadratic equation
obtained from (13) by straightforward arithmetic

$$- \lambda^2 [\frac{1}{x_o x_1 \mu_o^2 \mu_1} + \frac{1}{x_o x_1 \mu_o \mu_1^2} + \frac{\sigma_o^2}{x_o x_1 \mu_1} + \frac{\sigma_1^2}{x_o x_1 \mu_o}$$

$$+ \frac{2(\tau - \frac{1}{\mu_o} - \frac{1}{\mu_1})}{x_o x_1 \mu_o \mu_1}] + \lambda [\frac{1}{x_o \mu_o^2} + \frac{\sigma_o^2}{x_o} + \frac{1}{x_1 \mu_1^2}$$

$$+ \frac{\sigma_1^2}{x_1} + 2(\tau - \frac{1}{\mu_o} - \frac{1}{\mu_1})(\frac{1}{x_o \mu_o} + \frac{1}{x_1 \mu_1})] = 2(\tau - \frac{1}{\mu_o} - \frac{1}{\mu_1})$$

Multiplying both sides by $-x_o x_1$ yields

$$a\lambda^2 - (bx_o + cx_1)\lambda = -dx_o x_1 \tag{14}$$

with

$$a = \frac{1}{\mu_o^2 \mu_1} + \frac{\sigma_o^2}{\mu_1} + \frac{1}{\mu_o \mu_1^2} + \frac{\sigma_1^2}{\mu_o} + 2\,\frac{\tau - \frac{1}{\mu_o} - \frac{1}{\mu_1}}{\mu_o \mu_1} > 0$$

$$b = \frac{1}{\mu_1^2} + \sigma_1^2 + 2(\tau - \frac{1}{\mu_o} - \frac{1}{\mu_1})\frac{1}{\mu_1} > 0 \tag{15}$$

$$c = \frac{1}{\mu_o^2} + \sigma_o^2 + 2(\tau - \frac{1}{\mu_o} - \frac{1}{\mu_1})\frac{1}{\mu_1} > 0$$

$$d = 2(\tau - \frac{1}{\mu_o} - \frac{1}{\mu_1}) > 0$$

Equation (18) is solved by

$$\lambda = \frac{bx_o + cx_1}{2a} \pm \frac{1}{2a}\sqrt{(bx_o + cx_1)^2 - 4adx_o x_1} \tag{16}$$

By nature of a production function

$$\lambda(0, x_1) = \lambda(x_o, 0) = 0$$

This implies the minus sign for the square root. In terms of standardized variables

$$q_o = \frac{b}{a}x_o \qquad\qquad q_1 = \frac{c}{a}x_1 \tag{17}$$

equation (16) assumes the simple form

$$\lambda = \frac{q_o + q_1}{2} - \frac{1}{2}\sqrt{(q_o+q_1)^2 - 4\delta q_o q_1} \qquad (18)$$

This is a universal production function for case work in standardized form. It depends on only one parameter δ whose effects will now be studied. First observe that

$$\delta = \frac{ad}{bc} \leqslant 1 \qquad (19)$$

is necessary and sufficient for (18) to be real valued. It may be shown by a straightforward but tedious calculation that condition (16) is necessary and sufficient for the radicand in (18) to be positive for all q_o, q_1. Notice that $\lambda(q_o,q_1) \geqq 0$ and $=$ only when $q_o = 0$ or $q_1 = 0$. Moreover,

$$2\frac{\partial \lambda}{\partial q_i} = 1 - \frac{(1_o+q_1) - 2\delta q_j}{(q_o+q_1)^2 - 4\delta q_o q_1} > 0 \quad \text{for} \quad \delta < 1 \qquad (20)$$

$$2\frac{\partial^2 \lambda}{\partial q_i^2} = -(q_o+q_1)^2 - 4\delta q_o q_1 + \frac{(q_o+q_1 - 2\delta q_j)^2}{(q_o+q_1)^2 - 4\delta q_o q_1}$$

$$= \frac{4\delta(\delta-1)q_j^2}{(q_o+q_1)^2 - 4\delta q_o q_1} < 0 \quad \text{for} \quad \delta < 1 \qquad (21)$$

so that the law of diminishing returns applies. Notice, however, that the Hessian is singular since λ is linear homogeneous in x_o, x_1.

The parameter δ which determines the form of the law of diminishing returns is given by

$$\delta = \frac{bc}{ad} = \frac{[\frac{1}{\mu_o^2} + \sigma_o^2 + 2(\tau-\tau^*)][\frac{1}{\mu_1^2} + \sigma_1^2 + \tau^*]}{\tau^* \cdot [\frac{1}{\mu_o \mu_1} + \frac{\sigma_o^2}{\mu_1} + \frac{1}{\mu_o^2 \mu_1} + \frac{\sigma_1^2}{\mu_o} + \frac{\tau^*}{\mu_o \mu_1}]}$$

where
$$\tau^* = 2(\tau - \frac{1}{\mu_o} - \frac{1}{\mu_1}) \tag{22}$$

measures the tightness of the delay constraint. A straight-forward calculation yields

$$\delta = 1 - \frac{(\frac{1}{\mu_o^2} + \sigma_o^2)(\frac{1}{\mu_1^2} + \sigma_1^2)}{(\frac{1}{\mu_o^2} + \sigma_o^2 + \frac{\tau^*}{\mu_o})(\frac{1}{\mu_1^2} + \sigma_1^2 + \frac{\tau^*}{\mu_1})} \tag{23}$$

Thus the tighter the delay constraint, <u>ceteris paribus</u>, the smaller is δ

$$\frac{\partial \delta}{\partial \tau^*} > 0. \tag{24}$$

Now observe that

$$\frac{\partial \lambda}{\partial \delta} = \frac{4 q_o q_1}{(q_o + q_1)^2 - 4\delta q_o q_1} > 0 \tag{25}$$

relaxing the time constraint increases output.

$$\frac{\partial^2 \lambda}{\partial q_i \partial \delta} > 0, \tag{26}$$

relaxing the time constraint increases the marginal product of supervisors and case workers. Moreover, the elasticity of substitution between x_o and x_1 increases with δ and τ^*.

As τ^* is relaxed completely output assumes its upper bound

$$\lim_{\tau^* \to \infty} \lambda = \lim_{\delta \to 1} \lambda = \frac{q_o + q_1}{2} - \frac{1}{2}\sqrt{(q_o - q_1)^2} = \text{Min} (q_o, q_1) \tag{27}$$

since the right-hand expression in (27) is either q_o or q_1. Thus the maximal stationary flow of cases is limited by the smaller of the two capacities of operatives and supervisors.

Introducing the new variables

$$v = \frac{\lambda}{x_1} = \text{output per supervisor}$$

$$u = \frac{x_0}{x_1} = \text{span of control}$$

then equation (16) assumes the form

$$v = \frac{c}{2a} + \frac{b}{2a} u - (\frac{c}{2a} + \frac{b}{2a} u)^2 - \frac{du}{a}$$

$$v = \alpha + \beta u - (\alpha + \beta u)^2 - \gamma u \tag{28}$$

$$\alpha = \frac{c}{2a} > 0 \quad \beta = \frac{b}{2a} > 0 \quad \gamma = \frac{d}{a} > 0 \quad \gamma = 4\alpha\beta$$

Equation (28) shows how output per supervisor increases with his/her span of control. This increase is subject to the law of diminishing returns, as demonstrated above.

It may be asked why case work requires an organization, why it should not be handled by individual case workers acting independently on their own? Presumably some kind of supervision is required to insure _conformity_ with standards and _uniformity_ in the application of criteria. Organization is here needed for _technical_ rather than economic reasons.

We may elaborate this important point as follows. Certain tasks cannot be performed by individuals on their own but require team work or collaboration of several persons. Examples are those jobs that require "checking" by another person as in case work, in scientific research, in financial business deals, etc. This checking could be done on a contractual basis by outside controllers, but when the volume of business is large enough it is cheaper to combine agents and controllers in an organization. The controlling function is then naturally associated with supervision.

12 Information Costs: Research Teams

In journals like "Physical Review Letters" announcements of research results are published to assure priority. It has been observed that the list of authors occasionally takes up half the space of the entire announcement. In particular in physics, the enormous cost of the capital equipment seems to call for a human effort of comparable magnitude in each project. Technical conditions have generated research teams that may contain several dozen high caliber technicians and scientists.

In the theoretical branches of social science by contrast the lone researcher aided by one or two assistants or the small team of two or more "principal investigators" still predominates. Is this a sign of the backwardness of social science? What in fact determines the optimal size of a research team? The present paper does not purport to come up with numerical answers to this question--except by way of illustration based on casual empiricism. But it attempts to probe into the factors that govern the optimal size or "optimal span of control" in the execution of research. It must be sharply distinguished from the optimal span of control in the administration of research. The latter is done in upper ranks by officials who--as they would be the first to admit--are no longer researchers themselves.

The following analysis will be focused on the type of theoretical research that is characteristic of the social sciences, but to some extent still exists in the physical sciences as well. No specialized equipment for experiments is assumed. The researcher requires as the only physical tools no more than the library and the computer. The use of these inputs by a rational researcher will be governed by the same principles that apply to resource use by any rational agent: the last hour spent with either the computer or the library resources must yield the same returns as the last hour spent by the researcher on his/her own. When the marginal product of either factor is below that level even initially, that factor will simply not be used.

It is the use of another resource that one is concerned with in studying optimal team size, and that is the resource "fellow researcher": the interaction with others yielding information, stimulation, criticism and encouragement received through time spent with collaborators.

One style of team research--and the only one that I have experienced at first hand--consists in frequent, often daily, conferences with one or two co-workers or sometimes the entire team while "hacking out" a problem. Such a session may be initiated spontaneously when one of the team members has had an "idea" to be tried out on the others. This idea will in most cases be shot down; or it may be subjected to revision, modification and/or elaboration. In the exposition and discussion among colleagues ideas must prove their worth or be set aside. Occasionally a new idea may be born in the course of such a discussion. However, such periods of live interaction must be interspersed with times when researchers work on their own. This time is needed not only for the absorption of information--from the literature or from discussion with colleagues. It is also essential for the footwork that is required in research: The calculations that may be involved and the writing up of the semi-finished or final product. Last and not least for many researchers these quiet times are the seed-bed for the spawning of research ideas.

An individual researcher in a team does not have complete freedom of choice regarding the amount of time he or she wishes to spend alone in these pursuits. If the team is to function properly a team member must make himself/herself available to the others upon request. The total amount of time a person has on his/her own is thus dictated in large part by the number of persons who can call on him/her, i.e., the size of the research team.

12.1 Model

To formalize these notions let 1+x be the size of the team including the team leader. The special role of the team leader will not be explored in this paper. Rather we treat the team leader like any other team member. Each team member has interactions with x other researchers. He/she can call on them for their expertise and support. On the other hand, any of them may call on him/her. If it is true that ideas are spawned while team members are thinking on their own, then a person's productivity will be governed by two factors

. time available on one's own

. access to knowledge and skill of other team members.

We standardize total working time at unity. The demands $a(x)$ of the x others are an increasing function of x. Time available for thinking on one's own is then

$$1 - a(x)$$

$$\tag{1}$$

$$a'(x) > 0$$

The output of a researcher may be considered an increasing function of available research time (1) and of access to the x others. How does access to others affect productivity? Let us standardize the productivity of a person when on his/her own at unity. Then the productivity per hour resulting from interaction with x others is an increasing function of x to be written

$$1 + b(x)$$

$$b' > 0$$

A person's output   q   is assumed to be the algebraic product of available time and productivity per unit time

$$q = q(x) = \{1 - a(x)\} \{1 + b(x)\} \tag{2}$$

Without a team a person's output is unity. It is not unreasonable to assume that each other team member has a constant claim on one's time. Each team member can call with constant probability a meeting in which all participate or a one-on-one conference with oneself. This means

$$a(x) = a \cdot x \tag{3}$$

Similarly we will linearize   b(x)

$$b(x) = bx \tag{4}$$

This results in a production function for individual output

$$q(x) = \{1 - ax\}\{1 + bx\} \tag{5}$$

It is reasonable to assume

$$0 < a < 1 \quad 0 < b < 1 \tag{6}$$

A team is worth forming if

$$\frac{dq(x)}{dx} > 0 \quad \text{for} \quad x = 0.$$

This implies

$$a < b \tag{7}$$

When $x = \frac{1}{a}$ other persons are in the team then there is no time left for individual work: productivity is zero. In between there is clearly a team size resulting in maximal individual productivity.

12.2 Production Function

How is individual output to be aggregated into team output? In a typical project the team leader divides the project into subtasks and assigns responsibility for these to individual team members. Members work on their assignments with the assistance of other team members. It is assumed once more that the actual research is done by individuals. It does not matter here whether progress is achieved during discussions or during time on one's own.

The team output is then the sum of the outputs of individuals, just as the whole is the sum of the parts assigned to the individuals. This output $Q(x)$ is then $x+1$ times the output of a representative individual.

At this point a distinction could be introduced between two types of team leaderships: directing or participating. In the first case the team leader does not assign to himself/herself one particular subtask; in the later he/she does. The team leader may even assign the writing of introduction and conclusions to some team member, but typically feels responsible himself/herself for this important subtask.

Here we will assume that the team leader contributes a subtask like everyone else so that

$$Q(x) = (1+x)(1 - ax)(1 + bx) \tag{8}$$

This output is a cubic function of x

$$Q(x) = 1 + (1+b-a)x + (b-a-ab)x^2 - abx^3 \qquad (9)$$

It is graphed in Figure 12.1 for $a = \dfrac{1}{10}$

$$b = \dfrac{1}{5}$$

This function exhibits all the properties of a classical production function. Initially it has positive and increasing returns (to substitution), later diminishing and finally negative marginal products of labor.

$$Q'(x) = 1 + b - a + 2(b-a-ab)x - 3abx^2 \qquad (10)$$

$$Q''(x) = 2(b-a-ab) - 6abx \qquad (11)$$

Notice that $Q(x)$ is initially convex and subsequently concave in view of (6), (7), (11).

$$Q(x) = (1+x)(1 - ax)(1 + bx); \quad A = 0.1, \quad B = 0.2$$

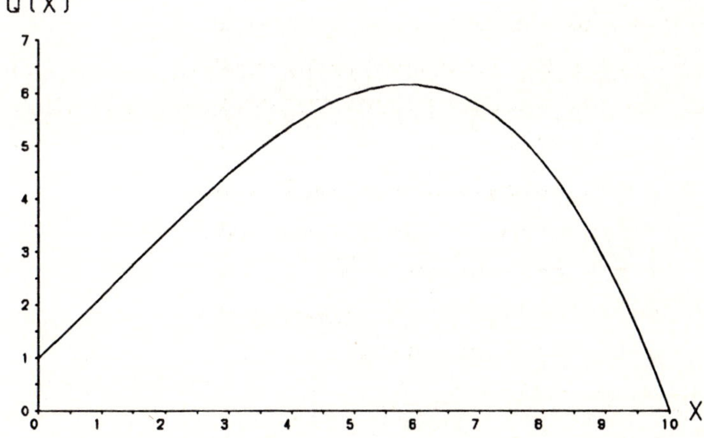

Figure 12.1.   Production Function of Research Teams

12.3 Checking

As another example suppose that supervision consists in checking and correcting the work of subordinates. The probability of detecting a hidden object through random search considered as a function of search effort (in time units) t is

$$1 - e^{-\delta t} \tag{1}$$

where $\delta \Delta t$ is the detection probability during a small time interval Δt.

Suppose further that with probability p work of a subordinate contains a serious flaw, reducing the value of the subordinate's output by a factor a, $0 < a < 1$. The expected value of the subordinate's output without supervision is then

$$q = 1-p + p(1-a) = 1-pa \tag{2}$$

If X_1 managers allocate an amount $b \leqslant 1$ of time to checking the work of X_0 operatives, the effective search time t in (1) equals

$$t = b \, \frac{X_1}{X_0} \tag{3}$$

Suppose the detection and correction of the error reduces the loss from a to $c < a$, then (2) is modified as follows:

$$q = 1 - pc \cdot (1-e^{-\delta t}) - pae^{-\delta t}$$

$$= 1 - pc - p \cdot (a-c) \, e^{-\delta t}$$

$$= 1 - pc - p(a-c) \, e^{-b\delta \, X_1/X_0}$$

The organization's output as a function of the two inputs of labor X_0 and management X_1 is then

$$y = X_0 \cdot [1 - pc - p(a-c)\, e^{-\delta b\, X_1/X_0}]$$

This is the production function that applies when management's principal task is checking. By construction it is linear homogeneous. Figure 12.2 shows an example with $a = 1$ $p = \frac{1}{4}$ $c = 0,\quad \delta b = 1$

$$y = X_0\, [1 - \tfrac{1}{4}\, e^{-\, X_1/X_0}]$$

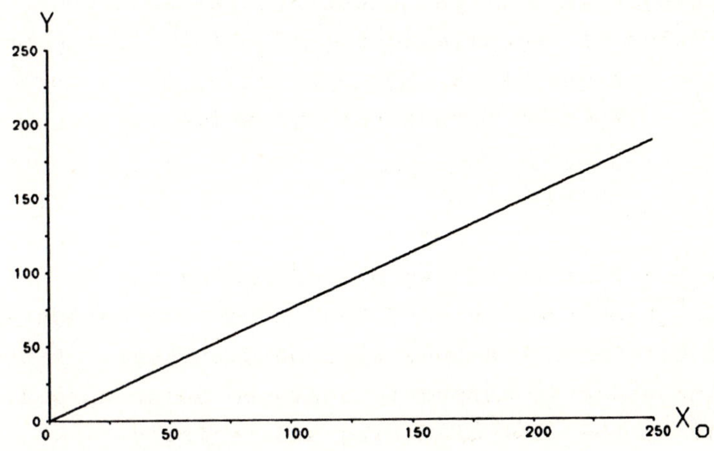

Figure 12.2. Production Function for Checking

13 Loss of Information in Simple Organizations

13.1 <u>Setting Targets</u>

Under perfect management the supervisor knows what to expect from every one of his/her subordinates. Under imperfect information only a probability distribution is known for the achievement potential of a "representative operative" under one's supervision. This distribution will be less precise, have larger variance, the greater the number of subordinates is under one supervisor, i.e., the greater the span of control $\dfrac{x_0}{x_1}$.

How should the supervisor set targets? If too low, the capabilities of operatives are underutilized. If too high, then those who cannot meet targets must be dismissed under the usual operating rules of organizations. If $P(u)$ is the probability distribution for output u per operative, and a target x is set, then the expected output per operative is

$$x\{1 - P(x)\} \qquad\qquad (1)$$

Here we assume that those capable of producing $u > x$ will not produce more than required and that those who cannot achieve x contribute nothing since they will be dismissed. Alternatively, we may count whatever output is achieved below target x as an offset against the cost of firing and rehiring.

We wish to determine the optimal target level x in (1) and the expected output achieved, and study its dependence on the number n of persons under one supervisor or manager. To choose the simplest scenario let $P(u)$ be the uniform distribution with expected value 1 and range 2a.

$$P(u) = \frac{u - 1 + a}{2a} \qquad 1-a \leqslant u \leqslant 1+a \qquad (2)$$

where the half range a is also the standard deviation and is restricted to

$$0 < a \leq 1 \qquad (3)$$

A necessary condition for a maximum of (1) is

$$0 = \frac{d}{dx} (x \{1 - P(x)\}) = 1 - P(x) - x\, p(x)$$

where

$$p(x) = \frac{dP}{dx}$$

For the uniform distribution (2) we seek

$$v = \frac{1}{2a} \; \underset{x}{\text{Max}} \; x \{1 + a - x\}$$

which is found to be

$$x = \frac{1+a}{2} \qquad (4)$$

and equals

$$v = \frac{1}{8} \frac{(1+a)^2}{a} = \frac{1}{8} (a + 2 + \frac{1}{a}) \qquad (5)$$

Under the restriction (3), v is indeed a decreasing function of the standard deviation a.

This standard deviation a must be an increasing function of n and be restricted to the range (3). As an illustration we choose

$$a(n) = \frac{1}{1+n^{-\frac{1}{2}}} \tag{6}$$

which for $n = 1,2, \ldots$ increases from $\frac{1}{2}$ to 1. We consider the output $y(n)$ of n operatives under one manager.

$$y(n) = n \cdot \frac{1}{8} \left\{ a(n) + 2 + \frac{1}{a(n)} \right\}$$

$$y(n) = \frac{1}{8} \frac{n}{1+n^{-\frac{1}{2}}} + \frac{3}{8} n + \frac{1}{8} n^{\frac{1}{2}} \tag{7}$$

This output function $y(n)$ defines an organizational production function for the output of x_1 simple organizations with managers and

$$n = \frac{x_0}{x_1}$$

operatives each

$$f(x_0,x_1) = x_1 \cdot y\left(\frac{x_0}{x_1}\right) \tag{8}$$

This production function is linear homogeneous by construction. In Figure 3.1 the output function $y(n)$ is graphed. It is initially convex and then concave.

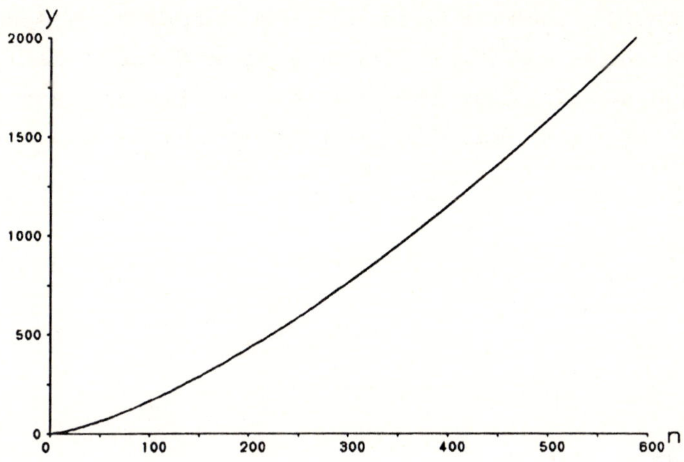

Figure 13.1. Output Function

Consider also the problem of finding the optimal span of control when an operative's wage w is given and the manager receives the surplus. The manager's surplus is then

$$g = \operatorname*{Max}_{n} \left\{ y(n) - wn \right\} \tag{9}$$

or

$$= \operatorname*{Max}_{n} \left\{ \frac{1}{8} \frac{n}{1+n^{-\frac{1}{2}}} + \frac{1}{8} n^{\frac{1}{2}} + \left(\frac{3}{8} - w\right) n \right\}$$

A necessary condition is

$$\frac{1 + \frac{3}{2} n^{-\frac{1}{2}}}{((1+n)^{-\frac{1}{2}})^2} + \frac{1}{2} n^{-\frac{1}{2}} - \lambda \, (8w-3) = 0 \tag{10}$$

For $w = \frac{145}{228}$, one obtains an optimal span of control

$$n = \frac{x_0}{x_1} = 4 \quad \text{(cf. Figure 13.2)}.$$

This example demonstrates how the output of a simple organization shows (at first increasing and then) decreasing returns which result from the loss of information about the capabilities of each subordinate that arises as their number is increased.

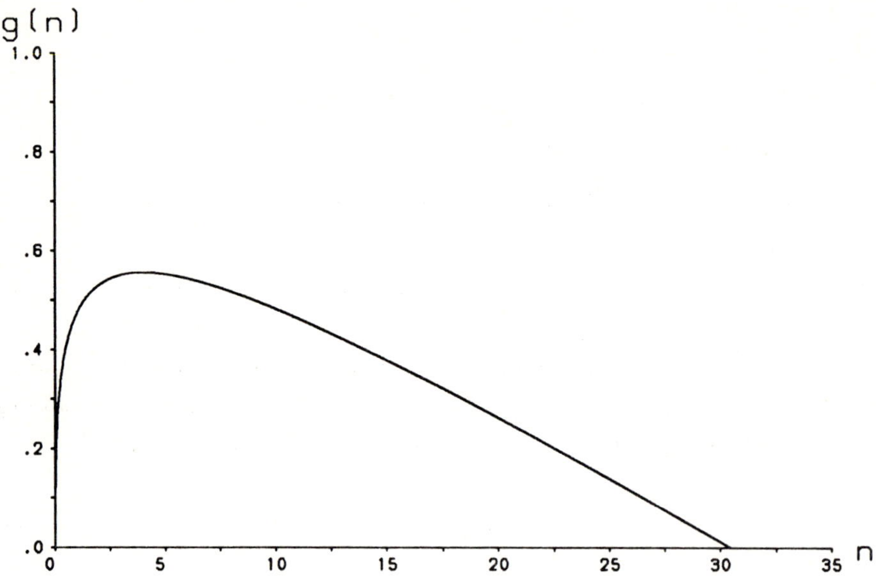

Figure 13.2. Profit Function

13.2 Budgeting with Full Information

One of the principal functions of the manager of a simple organization or team is to allocate resources to the various team members, specifically funds. Each team member's product will be described by a production function, let us say Cobb-Douglas function of the following type

$$y_i = b_i \, m_i^{\beta} \qquad 0 < \beta < 1$$

i   Index of team member

b_i a coefficient measuring the productivity of group member i
in his assigned task

β output elasticity common to all members

m_i funds allocated to i

m $= \sum_i m_i$ total funds available

In the absence of a manager, when each member receives the same fund $m_i = \frac{m}{n}$ total output is

$$y_0 = \left(\frac{m}{n}\right)^\beta \cdot \sum_{i=1}^{n} b_i \tag{11}$$

Let b_i be a random variable with expected value μ. When $b_i \equiv \mu$ the expected output of n individuals each receiving funds $\frac{m}{n}$ equals

$$y_0 = n\, Ey_i = n\mu\left(\frac{m}{n}\right)^\beta = \mu n^{1-\beta} m^\beta \tag{12}$$

and this is a Cobb-Douglas function in terms of total personnel n and total funds m.

Assume that the manager knows all b_i with certainty. His allocation problem requires

$$\underset{m_i}{\text{Max}} \sum_{i=1}^{n} b_i\, m_i^{\beta} \tag{13}$$

such that

$$\sum_{i=1}^{n} m_i \leq m \tag{14}$$

Maximizing a Lagrange function

$$L = \sum_i b_i \, m_i^{\beta} + \lambda \left\{ m - \sum_i m_i \right\}$$

yields

$$\beta \, b_i \, m_i^{\beta-1} = \lambda$$

$$m_i = \left\{ \frac{\beta b_i}{\lambda} \right\}^{\frac{1}{1-\beta}} \tag{15}$$

Substituting in (15)

$$m = \sum_i m_i = \lambda^{-\frac{1}{1-\beta}} \, \beta^{\frac{1}{1-\beta}} \left\{ \sum_i b_i \right\}^{\frac{1}{1-\beta}}$$

and substituting this in (14) we have

$$m_i = \frac{b_i^{\frac{1}{1-\beta}}}{\sum_j b_j^{\frac{1}{1-\beta}}} \, m \tag{16}$$

The budget share of operative i should be made equal to the share of his amplified productivity

$$b_i^{\frac{1}{1-\beta}}$$

in the sum of these terms.

The resulting output is then

$$y = \{ \sum_{j=n}^{n} b_j^{\frac{1}{1-\beta}} \}^{1-\beta} \, m^{\beta} \tag{17}$$

When all b_j are equal to μ then (17) agrees with (12).
When the b_j are different, then

<u>Proposition</u>: Suppose the b_j are known and different and funds
are optimally allocated according to (16). Then achieved output
(17) exceeds the output under an equal allocation

$$y = \{ \sum_{i=1}^{n} b_i^{\frac{1}{1-\beta}} \}^{1-\beta} m^{\beta} > \{ \frac{1}{n} \sum_{i=1}^{n} b_i \} n^{1-\beta} m^{\beta} = y_0 \tag{18}$$

<u>Proof</u>: For $0 \leqslant \beta < 1$ $\quad b^{\frac{1}{1-\beta}}$ is a convex function of b.
Jensen's inequality (Beckenbach and Bellman, 1961) for convex
functions states that

$$\left(\frac{\sum\limits_{i=1}^{n} b_i}{n} \right)^{\frac{1}{1-\beta}} \leqslant \frac{1}{n} \sum_{i=1}^{n} b_i^{\frac{1}{1-\beta}} \tag{19}$$

and "=" only when $b_i \equiv b$. Hence if the b_i are different,
taking (19) to the power $1-\beta$ and multiplying by $m^{\beta} > 0$ yields
(18). $\|$

Since the inequality (18) is strict unless all $b_i \equiv$
constant, a manager's productivity in budgeting results from
his/her knowledge where funds are best applied.

Suppose for instance that the b_i are random variables uniformly distributed in the interval $0 \leqslant b \leqslant 2$. An operative on his/her own operating with a budget of $m = 1$ would then achieve b_i and therefore on average an output of unity.

The expected value of output under a manager is then

$$y = E\{ \sum_{i=1}^{n} b_i^{\frac{1}{1-\beta}} \}^{1-\beta} \cdot m^{\beta} = m^{\beta} \cdot n^{1-\beta} \cdot \{ \frac{1}{2} \int_0^2 x^{\frac{1}{1-\beta}} dx \}^{1-\beta}$$

Now

$$(\frac{1}{2} \int_0^2 x^{\frac{1}{1-\beta}} dx)^{1-\beta} = 2^{\beta-1} (\frac{1-\beta}{(2-\beta)} \cdot 2^{\frac{2-\beta}{1-\beta}})^{1-\beta} = 2(\frac{1-\beta}{2-\beta})^{1-\beta}$$

$$= 2 \cdot (\frac{3/4}{7/4})^{3/4} = 1.0593694 \quad \text{for} \quad \beta = \frac{1}{4}$$

Then

$$y = 1.0597694 \ m^{\beta} n^{1-\beta}$$

and if $m = n$

$$y = 1.0593694 \ n$$

compared to an expected output of n under an equal allocation. The manager's marginal product is therefore

$$w_1 = .0593694 \cdot n$$

$$> 1 \quad \text{for} \quad n \geqslant 17$$

To earn a salary above the unit wage of an operative, the manager should supervise at least 17 operatives.

Of course, a manager performs other functions besides budgeting and may thus profitably supervise fewer than 17 operatives.

13.3 Incomplete Information

We turn now to a consideration of the effect of the span of control on the manager's information.

Suppose that the manager estimates person i's productivity coefficient to be μ_i and that this estimate is unbiased.

$$\mu_i = E\, b_i$$

the allocation based on this estimate is expected output of

$$\hat{y} = Ey = E \sum b_i \left(\frac{\mu_i^{\frac{1}{1-\beta}}}{\sum_j \mu_j^{\frac{1}{1-\beta}}} \right)^\beta$$

$$\hat{y} = \left\{ \sum_i \mu_i^{\frac{1}{1-\beta}} \right\}^{1-\beta} \tag{19}$$

The output under perfect knowledge would have been (17).

Compare now the expected value of output (17) under perfect information with the output achieved by a manager acting under imperfect information (19) where $\beta = \frac{1}{2}$

$$\Delta = E\left(\sqrt{\sum_i b_i^2} - \sqrt{\sum_i \mu_i^2} \right)$$

$$\Delta = E\left(\sqrt{\sum_i (\mu_i^2 + \sigma_r^2)} - \sqrt{\sum_i \mu_i^2} \right)$$

where σ_r^2 is the remaining variance of b_i under the estimate μ_i. If all i have the same expected performance parameter μ, $E\,\mu_i = \mu$, then this becomes

$$\Delta = \sqrt{n}\,\left\{\sqrt{\mu^2 + \sigma_r^2} - \mu\right\} \tag{20}$$

This is the expected shortfall of output under a manager whose estimates μ_i of performance characteristics are subject to an error with variance σ_r^2.

Now the expected output per unit of funds under perfect information is

$$E\,\sqrt{\sum b_i^2} = \sqrt{n}\cdot\sqrt{\mu^2 + \sigma^2}$$

where σ^2 is the total variance of b_i.

A manager's output per unit of funds is therefore

$$\frac{y}{\sqrt{m}} = \sqrt{n}\cdot\left\{\sqrt{\mu^2 + \sigma^2} + \mu - \sqrt{\mu^2 + \sigma_r^2}\right\} \tag{21}$$

Now the error variance σ_r^2 of a manager is itself dependent on the number n of subordinates, say

$$\sigma_r^2 = \sigma^2\left(1 - \frac{1}{n}\right) \tag{22}$$

The production function of n persons under a manager administering funds m is then

$$F(m,n) = \sqrt{m}\,\sqrt{n}\,\left\{\mu + \sqrt{\mu^2 + \sigma^2} - \sqrt{\mu^2 + \sigma^2\left(1 - \frac{1}{n}\right)}\right\} \tag{23}$$

this function is graphed in Figure 3 for

$$m = 10.000$$

$$\mu = 10$$

$$\sigma^2 = 25$$

and various n.

It is seen that (23) is no longer homogeneous of degree one in m and n. Rather it shows diminishing returns to scale. If one unit of funds is used per operative and operatives are paid a wage of w and if $\mu = 1$ and $\sigma^2 = 1$ then the optimal number of subordinates--the optimal team size or span of control--is determined by

$$\underset{n}{\text{Max}} \ (1 + \sqrt{2} - \sqrt{2 - \frac{1}{n}})n - wn$$

$$y = \underset{n}{\text{Max}} \ (an - \sqrt{n^2 - \frac{n}{2}})$$

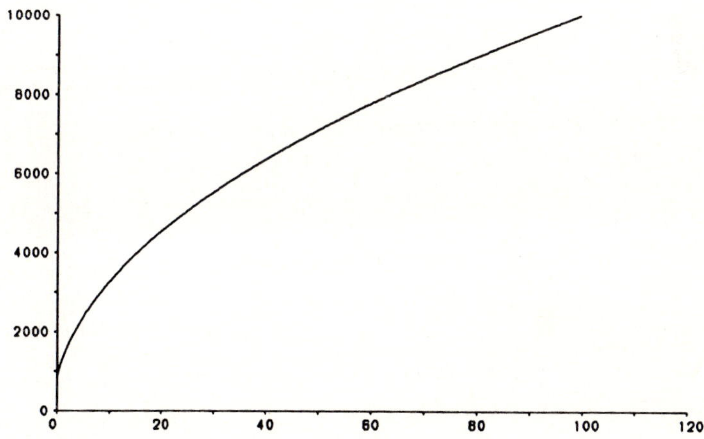

Figure 13.3. Output of n Persons with Fixed Total Budget

where

$$a = \frac{1 + \sqrt{2 - w}}{\sqrt{2}}$$

Optimization yields

$$n = \frac{1}{4} \left(1 + \frac{a}{\sqrt{a^2-1}}\right)$$

which is sensitive to w. A wage rate of

$$w = 1 - \frac{\sqrt{2}}{800} = 0.9982$$

implies $n^* = 10$.

These considerations suggest once more that managerial functions other than budgeting must be responsible for the limited span of control observed in practice. Nevertheless, budgeting imposes its own constraints on the scope of management.

14 Loss of Information and Control in Multi-Level Organizations

One reason frequently mentioned why R affects productivity in a negative way is that communication through many layers of an administrative hierarchy generates information that is filtered, outdated and/or distorted. Therefore, decisions by top management are not as effective as those under shorter lines of communication. This is formalized by the notion of control loss (Section 14.2). We examine first one principal cause for the loss of information.

14.1 Loss of Information

The higher is his/her rank, the closer a person is to the "center of things" in an organization, particularly for information originating with the president. Also the more removed is a person from information input by nonsupervisors (operatives).

If major decisions issue from the president's office then proximity to the center, measured by $R-r$ in counting down determines how soon and sometimes how much you know.

Filtering or dilution of information at some loss rate δ turns out to be necessary to prevent the system from being overloaded with information.

Consider an organization member i. From various other members j in a source set S_i, information μ_j (in bits, say) is received per unit of time, totalling $\sum\limits_{j \in S_i} \mu_j$.

This is filtered and processed yielding an amount of information

$$(1 - \delta_i) \sum\limits_{j \in S_i} \mu_j$$

In general, further information m_i is added. Information outflow is then

$$\mu_i - m_i + (1-\delta_i) \sum_{j \varepsilon S_i} \mu_j \tag{1}$$

and this is passed to all members k in a recipience set T_i, $k \varepsilon T_i$ continuing the process.

For all members i this flow must be kept below capacity, say unity $\mu_i \leq 1$. When official channels are used this can be made more specific. Let each supervisor have no more than s subordinates directly reporting to him/her and let each member filter the information received at a loss rate of at least δ and generate additional information at a rate not exceeding m. Then the rate μ_r of emission of information by a member of rank r in terms of the rate μ_{r-1} of information received from the s subordinates is restricted by

$$\mu_r \leq m + (1-\delta)s\mu_{r-1}. \tag{2}$$

Through successive substitution

$$\mu_r \leq m \cdot [1 + (1-\delta)s + (1-\delta)^2 s^2 + \ldots + (1-\delta)^r s^r]$$

$$= m \frac{1 - (1-\delta)^{r+1} s^{r+1}}{1 - (1-\delta)s}$$

or

$$\mu_r < \frac{m}{1 - (1-\delta)s} \tag{3}$$

A sufficient condition for this upward information flow to lie within the capacity 1 for information emission of any member is

$$\frac{m}{1 - (1-\delta)s} \leqslant 1$$

This may be expressed in three different ways.

$$m \leq 1 - (1-\delta)s \qquad\qquad (4)$$

or

$$\delta \geq 1 - \frac{1-m}{s} \qquad\qquad (5)$$

or

$$s \leq \frac{1-m}{1-\delta} \qquad\qquad (6)$$

Constraints (4), (5), and (6) are equivalent. Condition (4) limits the amount of information that can be generated when δ and s are given; condition (5) imposes a lower bound on the elimination rate δ for information, when m and s are given. Finally, condition (6) limits the span of control, when information generation m and elimination rate δ are given.

14.2 Loss of Control

As suggested by Williamson (1967) the effectiveness of labor is reduced by a factor of ρ^R, $0 < \rho < 1$ when top management is separated from labor by a chain of length R. Thus output Q and labor force L are related by

$$Q = \rho^R L \qquad\qquad (7)$$

In Section 6.3 the required size N of an organization employing operative labor L was shown to be

$$N = \frac{sL-1}{s-1} \qquad\qquad \text{from (6.3.4)}$$

$$= \frac{s\rho^{-R}Q-1}{s-1} \qquad\qquad \text{using (7),}$$

or dropping the 1

$$N \doteq \frac{\rho^{-R}}{1 - \frac{1}{s}} \cdot Q \tag{8}$$

To determine R observe that a constant span of control s implies

$$s^R = L = \rho^{-R}Q \qquad \text{or}$$

$$Q = (\rho s)^R \tag{9}$$

$$R = \frac{\ln Q}{\ln (\rho s)} \tag{10}$$

Substitute (10) in (8)

$$N = \frac{Q}{1 - \frac{1}{s}}\, e^{-R \ln \rho}$$

$$= \frac{1}{1 - \frac{1}{s}}\, Q e^{-\ln Q \cdot \frac{\ln \rho}{\ln \rho s}}$$

$$= \frac{1}{1 - \frac{1}{s}}\, Q^{1 - \frac{\ln \rho}{\ln \rho s}}$$

$$N = \frac{1}{1 - \frac{1}{s}}\, Q^{\frac{1}{n}} \tag{11}$$

where

$$\frac{1}{n} = 1 + \left| \frac{\ln \rho}{\ln \rho s} \right| > 1 \tag{12}$$

Observe that $\dfrac{1}{\eta} > 1$

Solving (11) for Q

$$Q = a \, N^{\eta} \quad \text{with} \quad \eta < 1 \tag{13}$$

This is Cobb-Douglas production function for output considered as a function of total personnel N as input. Notice that an exponent $\eta < 1$ would be consistent with the presence of another fixed factor, a hidden "management" component. In other words this model of control loss is formally identical with and cannot be distinguished from a Cobb-Douglas production function.

But is this control loss inevitable? Must it be taken as a technical constraint, or can it be considered an object of economic choice? In the latter case what is the optimal level of control loss that an organization should tolerate? This question is taken up in Chapter 19.

15 Uses of Production Functions: Simple Organizations

The examples of Chapter 11-14 produced linear homogeneous production functions. We consider first such linear homogeneous production functions and extend the results later to other cases.

15.1 Attainable Output

Output--or task size y--that is achievable with the organization's resources is described by a production function

$$y = F(x_0, x_1) \tag{1}$$

When a single organization is considered, $x_1 \leq 1$. Suppose that $x_1 > 1$ and x_1 integer. Now

$$F(x_0, x_1) = x_1 \ F(\frac{x_0}{x_1}, \ 1)$$

by linear homogeneity. Thus x_1 organizations can achieve x_1 times the output of a single organization with input $\frac{x_0}{x_1}$, 1. The converse statement is more interesting: since organizations can be duplicated, twice the output can always be achieved with twice of each input.

The linear homogeneous production function (1) may be rewritten

$$\frac{y}{x_0} = F(1, \ \frac{x_1}{x_0})$$

showing that the productivity of operatives depends on the inverse span of control $\dfrac{1}{s} = \dfrac{x_1}{x_0}$. Since F is an increasing function of each argument, an operative's productivity increases with the amount of supervision received x_1/x_0. This is in sharp contrast to the simple "constant span of control" condition that operative's productivity is constant so that output is a fixed multiple of operative labor as in Chapter 6.

15.2 Labor Requirements

The relationship between the three variables y, x_0, x_1 defined by the production function can be solved for x_0

$$x_0 = G(y, x_1) \quad \text{(say)}. \tag{2}$$

This states the operative labor required to handle a task of size y with x_1 supervisors. When the production function is bounded, then some outputs cannot be achieved with a given amount of managerial inputs, no matter how much operative labor x_0 is employed (see Figure 15.1).

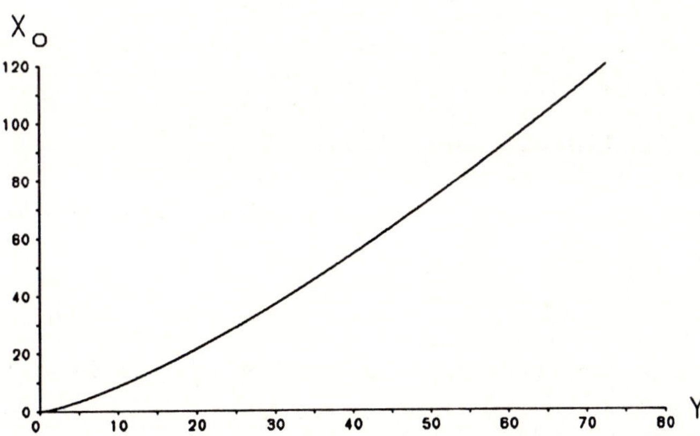

Figure 15.1.   Labor Requirements

When $x_1 \leq 1$ then (2) describes the operative requirements of a single organization; when $x_1 > 1$ and integer it states the combined operative labor input of x_1 simple organizations each

using $\dfrac{x_0}{x_1}$ operatives and producing $\dfrac{y}{x_1}$ units of output. For G

is also linear homogeneous

$$\frac{x_0}{x_1} = x_1 G\left(\frac{y}{x_1},\ 1\right)$$

15.3 Supervisory Input

Solving (1) for x_1

$$x_1 = H(y, x_0) \tag{3}$$

states the supervisory requirements for producing an output y with labor x_0. In the fixed span of control (or fixed coefficients) case we had

$$x_1 = \frac{y-1}{s-1} \qquad\qquad x_0 = y$$

where each input was a linear function of output y and there was no substitutability between x_0 and x_1.

Since H is linear homogeneous

$$\frac{x_1}{x_0} = H\left(\frac{y}{x_0},\ 1\right)$$

Supervisory input required per operative is now seen to be an increasing function of the productivity of an operative. For H in (3) is an increasing function of y and a decreasing function of x_0. (The reader should show this either directly by implicit differentiation of (1) or graphically by means of isoquants.)

When $x_1 > 1$ and integer, then (3) gives the number of simple organizations required to produce an output y with total operative labor x_0.

15.4 Minimizing the Cost of Given Output

Assume that wage rates w_r of operative labor x_0 and managerial labor x_1 are given and set in competitive labor markets. Then an organization can choose the mix of the two inputs that will achieve the task y at minimum cost $w_0 x_0 + w_1 x_1$. Mathematically

$$\underset{x_0, x_1}{\text{Min}} \quad w_0 x_0 + w_1 x_1 \tag{4}$$

subject to

$$F(x_0, x_1) = Q.$$

When F is linear homogeneous write

$$\frac{Q}{x_1} = y = F\left(\frac{x_0}{x_1}, 1\right) = f\left(\frac{x_0}{x_1}\right) = f(s)$$

$$w_1 = g \cdot w_0$$

and

$$w_0 x_0 + w_1 x_1 = w_0 x_1 \cdot \left(\frac{x_0}{x_1} + \frac{w_1}{w_0}\right) = w_0 x_1 \, (s+g)$$

In terms of the transformed variables, the minimum problem becomes

$$\underset{x_1, s}{\text{Min}} \quad w_0 x_1 \, (s+g) \tag{5}$$

subject to

$$x_1 f(s) = Q \tag{6}$$

Substituting x_1 from (6) in (5)

$$\underset{s}{\text{Min}} \quad \frac{s+g}{f(s)} \, w_0 Q$$

This is equivalent to finding

$$\underset{s}{\text{Max}} \quad \frac{f(s)}{s+g} \tag{7}$$

i.e., the maximum output per unit cost. The size Q of the task does not matter. Problem (7) is solved by

$$(s+g) \, f'(s) - f(s) = 0 \tag{8}$$

This equation may be written in terms of the output elasticity α of the production function f

$$\alpha = \frac{sf'}{f}$$

$$\frac{s}{s+g} = \alpha(s) \tag{8'}$$

Choose the span of control s to make $\dfrac{s}{s+g}$ equal to the output elasticity of operative labor. Implicit differentiation of (8) with respect to g yields

$$\frac{ds}{dg} = - \frac{f'}{(s+g)f''} > 0$$

since the production function is increasing and concave in the relevant range.

Thus the cost minimizing span of control is an increasing function of the wage ratio $\frac{w_1}{w_0}$. It is thus seen to be an economic variable, the result of an economic choice, rather than a technical coefficient.

Example: Cobb-Douglas Production Function

$$F(x_0, x_1) = bx_0^{\alpha} \, x_1^{1-\alpha}$$

The homogenized function is

$$y = bs^{\alpha}$$

Since the output elasticity $\alpha(s)$ is constant, we have from (8a)

$$\frac{s}{s+g} = \alpha$$

or

$$s = \frac{\alpha}{1-\alpha} \cdot g$$

Thus for Cobb-Douglas production functions, the span of control should be proportional to the salary span g.
With $g = \frac{4}{3}$ $\alpha = \frac{3}{4}$ this yields a span of control

$$s = 3 \cdot \frac{4}{3} = 4$$

15.5 Increasing Returns to Scale

Now let $F(x_0, x_1)$ be homogeneous of degree $m > 1$. Then

$$F(x_0, x_1) = x_1^m \, F(\frac{x_0}{x_1}, 1) \tag{1}$$

$$= x_1^m \, f(s) \qquad s = \frac{x_0}{x_1}$$

Under constant returns, the scale was arbitrary. Now we must observe that in a simple organization managerial input cannot exceed unity

$$x_1 \leqslant 1 \tag{2}$$

How large should a simple organization be in order to minimize average cost--or maximize average output?

$$
\begin{aligned}
\underset{\substack{x_1 \leqslant 1 \\ x_0}}{\text{Max}} \quad & \frac{F(x_0, x_1)}{g x_1 + x_0} \tag{3} \\[2ex]
= \underset{\substack{x_1 \leqslant 1 \\ s}}{\text{Max}} \quad & \frac{x_1^m\, f(s)}{x_1(g+s)} \\[2ex]
= \underset{x_1}{\text{Max}} \quad x_1^{m-1}\ \underset{s}{\text{Max}}\ & \frac{f(s)}{g+s} \\[2ex]
= \underset{s}{\text{Max}} \quad \frac{f(s)}{g+s} \qquad & x_1 = 1 \tag{4}
\end{aligned}
$$

since $m > 1$ and

$$\underset{0 \leqslant x \leqslant 1}{\text{Max}}\ x^{m-1} = 1$$

But (4) is identical with (15.4.7). We have thus reduced the problem to the same format as in the linear homogeneous case.

Production functions with initially increasing returns to scale will be considered once more in Chapter 17 when the advantages of simple organizations over individuals are considered.

16 Uses of Production Functions: Multi-Level Organizations

<u>16.1.A Production Function for Management</u>

The considerations of the last chapter will now be extended
to an organization with multiple levels of supervision.

The leading question is: how can the management process be
described in terms of inputs and outputs? We shall make use once
more of the concept of a production function familiar from the
description of the production of goods and services. The special
service produced in a management hierarchy is "management". It
is not directly observable but may be inferred from the final
product produced jointly by operatives and the inputs of
management at various levels.

Consider a multi-level organization and a representative
manager at level r. The supervisory effort achieved by the rth
level of management is itself a product of managerial labor at
that level and supervision from higher levels. At every level
r of management, except the president, we observe the following
schema

$$\frac{y_{r+1}}{x_r} \qquad \text{supervision by rank } r+1 \text{ of rank } r$$

managerial labor
    of rank = 1

$$\frac{y_r}{x_r} \qquad \text{supervision by rank } r \text{ of rank } r-1$$

Figure 11. <u>Schema of Managerial Control</u>

In the black box "supervision" or managerial control is produced from two inputs managerial labor at level r and supervision by level $r+1$.

The production unit is one office. The inputs are first one unit of labor, i.e., the time of a manager of rank r, and secondly a certain amount of supervision by higher level management. The output is supervision of managers at level $r-1$.

To quantify the inputs and outputs let x_r denote the managerial labor put in at level r. "Supervision" y is both an input and an output. Total supervision y_{r+1} produced at level $r+1$ is divided among the x_r officers of rank r so that each manager of rank r receives an amount $\dfrac{y_{r+1}}{x_r}$ of supervision. This plus one unit of managerial labor are the inputs into one office of rank r. Total supervision produced by officers of rank r is y_r. Per office we have therefore an output $\dfrac{y_r}{x_r}$.

The inputs into and output of a representative office of rank r is thus described by a relationship

$$\frac{y_r}{x_r} = F_r(1, \frac{y_{r+1}}{x_r})$$

We will call

$$y_r = x_r F_r(1, \frac{y_{r+1}}{x_r}) \tag{1}$$

a "management production function".

By construction this production function is linear homogeneous. With linear homogeneous f_r an equivalent statement of (1) is

$$y_r = f_r(x_r, y_{r+1}) \tag{1}$$

Supervision or "management" appears here as an intermediate product which cannot be observed directly. What is observable are the final output Q by the operatives at the lowest level r = 0, and the labor inputs x_r at all levels of the administrative hierarchy.

Notice that Figure 16.1 describes the input-output relationships for a single office. The management process described here may be called "management by delegation". Each office is working on its own but subject to control or supervision by higher levels.

An alternative would be "management by team work". This will be studied in the context of a simple organization involving only one supervisor and operatives (cf. Section 15). We have indexed the production function to indicate that it may depend on the level r. If one is willing to make the assumption that "management is management" and hence is the same operation at all levels, the production function may be considered to be independent of level r.

$$y_r = f(x_r, y_{r+1}) \tag{2}$$

At the lowest level y_0 represents the organization's output

$$y_0 = Q \tag{3}$$

and at the highest, the presidential level, there is no supervisory input, the president's input is his output.

$$y_R = x_R = 1 \tag{4}$$

Successive substitution in the recursive equation (2) yields an <u>organizational production function</u>

$$Q = f_0(x_0, f_1(x_1, \ldots, f_{R-1}(x_{R-1}, x_R) \ldots)) \qquad (5)$$

This is a nested production function. Since its building blocks f_r are all linear homogeneous, so is (5). When the presidential input is fixed at unity, then in terms of the remaining inputs the production function no longer exhibits constant return to scale but diminishing returns.

The special case of a Cobb-Douglas function has been studied in [Beckmann 1977]. The managerial production function has the form

$$\frac{y_r}{x_r} = b(r) \left(\frac{y_{r+1}}{x_r}\right)^\beta \qquad r = 1, \ldots, R-1 \qquad (9)$$

Notice that the output elasticities are assumed to be the same at all levels, but that the productivities $b(r)$ may vary. Equation (9) may be rewritten

$$y_r = b(r) \, x_r^\alpha \, y_{r-1}^\beta \qquad \alpha + \beta = 1 \qquad (10)$$

Nesting leads to the following organizational production function

$$Q = b(0)x_0^\alpha \, [b(1)x_1^\alpha [\cdots \, b(R-1)x_{R-1}^\alpha \, x_R^\beta]^\beta \, \ldots]^\beta$$

$$= b_R \prod_{r=0}^{R} x_r^{\alpha_r}$$

with

$$b_R = \prod_{r=0}^{R-1} b(r)^{\beta^r}$$

$$\alpha_r = \alpha\beta^r \qquad r = 0, \ldots, R-1$$

$$\alpha_R = \beta^R$$

With the simplifying assumption that the managerial Cobb-Douglas
functions are identical, the nested the organizational production
function becomes

$$Q = b^{1+\beta+\ldots+\beta^{R-1}} \prod_{r=0}^{R-1} x_r^{\alpha\beta^r} \cdot x_R^{\beta^r} \tag{11}$$

In view of $x_R = 1$ the last term $x_R^{\beta^R}$ may be dropped. The
organizational production function may now be used to study the
allocation of management resources in an organization.

16.2 Allocation of Inputs

In Chapter 6 the notion of efficiency has been introduced
and refined step by step

   i. The minimal number of supervisors required to
supervise the execution of a given task hence the
minimum number of personnel in the organization.

  ii. Avoidance of slack.

 iii. The minimum height of an organization consistent
with a given task.

  iv. the minimum average rank, minimum average wage cost,
and minimum unit labor cost.

These definitions were based on given constant spans of
control. In this section efficiency will be redefined as

Minimizing total salary cost incurred in achieving a given
task by choosing appropriate spans of control at each level.

As mentioned before other costs (rent of office space,
capital cost) could be included but this is not done here.

An alternative but equivalent efficiency concept is that for
a given budget B, the organization's output is maximized.

Since we are not concerned with the external problems of market structure, we assume perfect competition in the markets for labor of all administrative ranks r.

An important assumption is that salary of personnel depends only on the administrative level r. Thus we ignore salary increments due to length of service. Alternatively, we may consider a "representative" holder of a position or rank r whose salary may contain an average component due to length of service. But the principal part of salaries must be assumed to be determined by rank, in agreement with the analysis of Chapter 9.

16.3 Short Run

In the short run, only labor input at the operative level $r = 0$ can be changed. The production function is then, in effect,

$$Q = F(x_o, \bar{x}_1, \bar{x}_2, \ldots, \bar{x}_R) \tag{1}$$

with $\qquad x_r = \bar{x}_r \qquad r = 1, \ldots, R \tag{2}$

held constant for $r > 0$.

Inverting the monotone function $F(x_o, \ldots)$ yields

$$x_o = \phi(Q, \bar{x}_1, \bar{x}_2, \ldots, \bar{x}_R) \qquad (\text{say}). \tag{3}$$

As an example consider the case work production function

$$\frac{1}{\mu_o - \dfrac{Q}{x_o}} + \frac{1}{\mu_1 - \dfrac{Q}{\bar{x}_1}} = \tau \tag{4}$$

Its inverse is

$$x_o = \cfrac{1}{\mu_o - \cfrac{1}{\tau - \cfrac{1}{\mu_1 - \cfrac{Q}{\overline{x}_1}}}} \qquad (5)$$

This function is defined for $Q < \mu\overline{x}_1$ and is monotone increasing and convex.

Consider also a Cobb-Douglas production function

$$Q = a_R x_o^{\alpha_o} (\overline{x}_1)^{\alpha_1} (\overline{x}_2)^{\alpha_2} \ldots (\overline{x}_R)^{\alpha_R} \qquad \sum_{r=0}^{R} \alpha_r = 1 \qquad (6)$$

$$= a_R x_o^{\alpha_o} \qquad \text{(say)}.$$

The inverse is

$$x_o = [a_R^{-1} \ Q]^{\frac{1}{\alpha_o}} \qquad (7)$$

Now we introduce the cost function

$$C = \sum_{r=0}^{R} w_r x_r \qquad (8)$$

Observing (2), (3) this becomes

$$C = \sum_{r=1}^{R} w_r \overline{x}_r + w_o \ \phi(Q, \overline{x}_1, \ldots, \overline{x}_R)$$

$$= F + w_o x_o(Q) \qquad \text{(say)}$$

Thus in the Cobb-Douglas case

$$C = F + w_O \, [\overline{b}_R^{-1}]^{\frac{1}{\alpha_O}} \, Q^{\frac{1}{\alpha_O}} \tag{9}$$

Observe that the variable cost has constant elasticity. The elasticity coefficient is in fact $\frac{1}{\alpha_O}$, the inverse of the output elasticity α_O of operatives. In the case of a two-level case working organization with $\overline{x}_1 = 1$ the cost functions becomes

$$C = w_1 + \cfrac{w_O Q}{\mu_O - \cfrac{1}{\tau - \cfrac{1}{\mu_1 - Q}}}$$

This cost function is graphed in Figure 16.1 for $\mu_O = \mu_1 = 3$, $\tau = 1$, $w_O = 1$, $w_1 = 1.5$

$$C = 1.5 + \cfrac{Q}{3 - \cfrac{1}{1 - \cfrac{1}{3-Q}}}$$

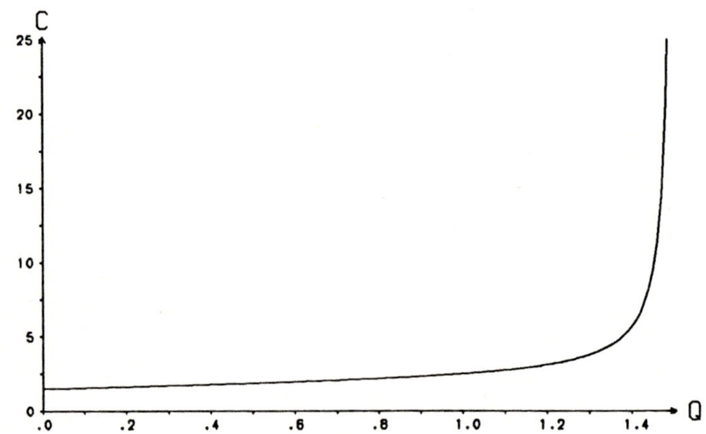

Figure 16.1.   Short-Run Cost Function

16.4 Medium Run: Optimal Spans of Control

In the medium run the organization can adjust personnel x_r at all levels r except the president's $r = 0, \ldots, R-1$, $\overline{x}_R = 1$.

The organization's production function is, therefore,

$$Q = F(x_o, x_1, \ldots, x_{R-1}, 1)$$

In the Cobb-Douglas case it is

$$Q = b_R \cdot x_o^{\alpha_o} \, x_1^{\alpha_1} \, \cdots \, x_{R-1}^{\alpha_{R-1}} \tag{1}$$

Obtaining the cost minimizing or efficient combinations of personnel x_r in the medium run in order to handle a given task Q is tantamount to finding the optimal spans of control

$$x_{r-1}/x_r, \qquad r = 1, \ldots, R.$$

Mathematically the problem is to determine

$$\text{Min} \sum_{r=0}^{R-1} w_r x_r + w_R \tag{2}$$

subject to production function (1).

Maximizing its Lagrangean

$$L = - \sum_{r=0}^{R} w_r x_r + \lambda \cdot [a_R \prod_{r=0}^{R-1} x_r^{\alpha_r} - Q] \tag{3}$$

yields

$$x_r = \lambda \cdot \frac{\alpha_r \, Q}{w_r} \tag{4}$$

Upon substituting (15) in the production function (1) one obtains

$$\lambda = b_R^{-\frac{1}{1-\alpha_R}} \; Q^{\frac{\alpha_R}{1-\alpha_R}} \; \prod_{r=0}^{R-1} \left(\frac{w_r}{\alpha_r}\right)^{\frac{\alpha_r}{1-\alpha_R}} \tag{5}$$

The span of control has the simple form

$$s_r = \frac{x_{r-1}}{x_r} = \frac{\alpha_{r-1}}{\alpha_r} \cdot \frac{w_r}{w_{r-1}} \qquad r = 1,\ldots,R-1 \tag{6}$$

This shows clearly how the span of control depends on relative wage rates.

This remarkable formula may be read in a slightly different way:

$$w_r = \frac{\alpha_r}{\alpha_{r-1}} \, s_r w_{r-1} . \tag{7}$$

Since $s_r w_{r-1}$ is the combined salary of those supervised (on the average) by an administrator level r, (7) states that the span of control should establish a proportional relationship between salaries of supervisors and those of the supervised [cf. Lydall, 1968].

In the case of identical Cobb-Douglas management production functions equation (6) shows that

$$s_r = \frac{1}{\beta} \, \frac{w_r}{w_{r-1}} \tag{8}$$

Once more, when salaries increase by a constant factor g

$$s_r = s = \frac{g}{\beta} \tag{9}$$

Equation (9) states that the average span of control should be constant at all levels r. This optimal span of control is proportional to the incremental salary factor g and inversely proportional to the output elasticity of supervision β.

Formula (9) permits to give rough estimates of α and β. If we accept as representative values

$$g = 1.25$$

$$s = 5$$

then

$$\beta = \frac{g}{s} = .25$$

This is in agreement with the estimated output elasticity of labor $\alpha = 75$ in general Cobb-Douglas production functions.

16.5 Medium Run: Cost Functions

Substitute now the recommended inputs (15) into the cost

$$C = \sum_{r=0}^{R} w_r x_r$$

to obtain

$$C = w_R + [1 - \alpha_R]\lambda Q$$

where we have used

$$\sum_{r=0}^{R} \alpha_r = 1$$

With the expression (16.4.5) substituted for λ one obtains

$$C = w_R + (1-\alpha_R)b_R^{\,-\frac{1}{1-\alpha_R}}\; Q^{\frac{1}{1-\alpha_R}}\; \prod_{r=0}^{R-1}\left(\frac{w_r}{\alpha_r}\right)^{\frac{\alpha_R}{1-\alpha_R}} \tag{1}$$

Once more, there is a fixed cost w_R and a variable cost whose elasticity is constant. The value of the elasticity

$$\eta = \frac{1}{1-\alpha_R} \tag{2}$$

is smaller than the short-run cost elasticity $\dfrac{1}{\alpha_O}$ since

$$\alpha_O < 1 - \alpha_R$$

in view of $\displaystyle\sum_{r=0}^{R}\alpha_r = 1$

Equation (2) states that the elasticity of variable cost with respect to output decreases with the number of levels R. In the special case of management production functions with identical exponents α,β one has $\alpha_R = \beta^R$ so that

$$\eta = \frac{1}{1-\beta^R}$$

which is clearly decreasing with respect to R.

Figure 16.2 shows some medium-run cost curves for $\alpha = \beta = \frac{1}{2}$ $a = 2.2,$ $w_r = \left(\frac{3}{2}\right)^r.$

16.6 Long Run: Optimal Number of Ranks

In the long run the level R of the organization may also be adjusted. The optimum level R which produces Q at minimum cost may be read off diagrams like Figure 16.2 or the appropriate cost curves that apply when the managerial production function is not Cobb-Douglas.

As the size of the task Q increases, so will the general number of levels R. This is best seen by comparing those outputs Q_R for which unit cost is minimized for given R.

A straightforward calculation for identical Cobb-Douglas production function yields [Beckmann, 1978, p. 128, equation (17)]

$$Q_R = a_R s_R^{1-\beta^R} s^{R + \frac{\beta^R - 1}{\alpha}} \tag{1}$$

Here s_R and s are determined by the salary scale. In particular for exponential wage scales $w_r = w_0 g^r$ it follows for large R since $\beta^R \to 0$, that

$$Q_R \doteq Q_0 \cdot s^R \tag{2}$$

where s is given by

$$s = \frac{g}{\beta}$$

Thus the output with minimum average cost increases exponentially with the organization's top rank R. The top rank R is strictly proportional to the logarithm of optimum output.

16.7 Long Run: Cost Functions

Another important question is how average cost or total cost varies with output. This topic will be taken up in fuller generality in Chapter 19.

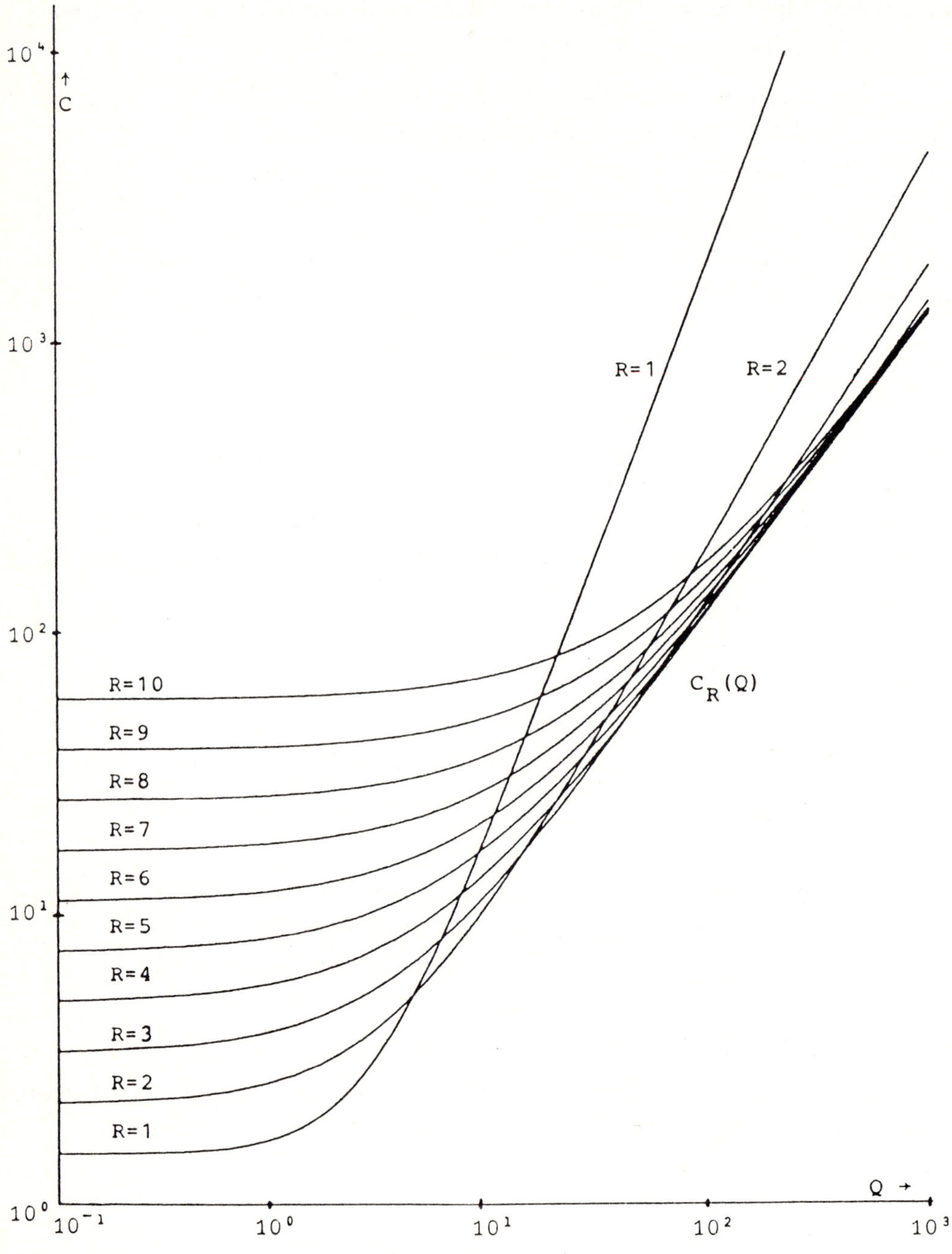

Figure 16.2.   Cost Curves for Different R

At this point we remark the following: When the management production functions are identical Cobb-Douglas

$$F_r(x_r, y_{r+1}) = b x_r^\alpha \, y_{r+1}^\beta \qquad \alpha + \beta = 1$$

then minimum unit cost for an organization with R levels achieved by an output Q_R as given in (24) is

$$c_R = w_o b^{-\frac{1}{\alpha}} \, g^{\frac{\beta}{\alpha}} \, \alpha^{-1} \beta^{-\frac{\beta}{\alpha}} \cdot [\frac{b g_R^\alpha}{g} \, \alpha^\alpha \beta^\beta]^{\frac{\beta}{\alpha}} \tag{3}$$

The conclusion is that this minimum unit cost is asymptotically constant, for

$$\lim_{r \to \infty} \beta^R = 0 \qquad \text{implies}$$

$$c_R \to w_o b^{-\frac{1}{\alpha}} \, g^{\frac{\beta}{\alpha}} \, \alpha^{-1} \beta^{-\frac{\beta}{\alpha}} \tag{4}$$

As R increases, the organizational production function, in which $x_R = 1$ is fixed, becomes asymptotically linear homogeneous. Consequently, minimum average cost becomes asymptotically constant.

17 Organizations versus Individuals

In Section 11 and elsewhere we have considered tasks that
can only be performed by organizations. But there are other
activities in which organizations compete with individuals. In
many areas it appears that organizations are in fact on the
advance. Increasingly they are taking over functions previously
performed mainly by individuals. Examples are the professions:

 lawyers and law firms,

 physicians and organized medical group practice

 management consultants and consulting firms

 operations research practitioners and operations

  research consulting businesses

 architects and architectural bureaus

 consulting engineers and engineering firms

 accountants and accounting firms, etc.

Writing and the fine arts seem to be almost the only fields
where individuals are still holding out against organizations.
But books have been authored by "authors' collectives" and great
paintings have come out of artists' workshops, e.g., of Rubens.
The marketing of art, however, has become an organized activity,
where galleries compete with artists' cooperatives and the
auction houses. What are the economic forces that permit and
drive this process? An economist will ask more specifically:
What is the economic advantage, if any, that an organization has
in doing jobs otherwise performed by indivdiuals? This is the
question studied in the present chapter. Chapter 20 compares two
basic types of organization: partnerships and organizations with
subordination and supervision. Chapter 19 examines how multi-
level organization or hierarchies proper can enter this

competition. In Section 17.4 we examine how personnel of different qualifications should be utilized by hierarchical organizations.

One assumption made throughout is that some operatives are also qualified to be supervisors or managers. One may even assume that everybody is equally qualified to be a manager (although this is neither realistic nor necessary). In that case one would add an assumption that management jobs require more effort than operative labor. It is a well-known fact that those who found organizations and manage them (entrepreneurs) put in longer working hours than do operatives. In addition, they place their own capital at risk, although this will not be considered here.

17.1 Organization of Individual Effort As pointed out above, organizations are a means of capturing economies of scale. Here we shall show, that only by doing so or by paying operatives less than their full opportunity wage--their earnings when independent--can they compete successfully against individuals on their own.

When comparing the output of organizations with that of individuals on their own, as e.g., in the professions, one must address the question of how inputs change as the result of "organization". Now organization has at least two aspects: specialization and supervision or "management". The need for management decreases the number of person units available for operative labor in an organization of n members. At the same time specialization should increase their productivity. The output of the organization as measured by an organizational production function should reflect both factors. The analysis of this section is in terms of simple organizations defined as involving only one level of supervision.

A person operating on his/her own is capable of producing (say) one unit of output per unit of time, valued at unity. Unity is, therefore, the opportunity wage of qualified personnel.

Even an individual on his/her own must allocate, however, some time to management functions, e.g., to the planning of work, to contacting customers, to decisions about capital equipment, etc. Thus if an amount x_0 is allocated to operative work and x_1 to management, the result will be

$$F(x_0, x_1).$$

The output y attainable with a total time input x is then given by

$$y = \max_{x_0 + x_1 \le x} F(x_0, x_1)$$

or

$$y = \phi(x), \qquad \text{say.} \tag{1}$$

By definition we have

$$\phi(0) = 0 \qquad \phi(1) = 1. \tag{2}$$

<u>Proposition 1.</u> Let $F(x_0, x_1)$ be homogeneous of degree m. Then

$$\phi(x) = x^m \quad \text{for all} \quad x \le 1$$

<u>Proof.</u> $\left(\dfrac{1}{x}\right)^m F(x_0, x_1) = F\left(\dfrac{x_0}{x}, \dfrac{x_1}{x}\right)$

$$\phi(x) = \max_{x_0 + x_1 = x} F(x_0, x_1)$$

$$= x^m \max_{\frac{x_0}{x} + \frac{x_1}{x} = 1} F\left(\frac{x_0}{x}, \frac{x_1}{x}\right)$$

Writing $\dfrac{x_0}{x} = u \qquad \dfrac{x_1}{x} = v$

$$\phi(x) = x^m \ \underset{\substack{u,v \\ u+v=1}}{\text{Max}} \ F(u,v)$$

$$= x^m \ \phi(1) = x^m \qquad\qquad ||$$

Therefore, if the combination of management and operative labor in one individual has returns to scale of constant degree $m > 0$, the resulting production function ϕ is a power function with exponent m. Consider the case of decreasing returns to scale $m < 1$. Suppose a unit of work is divided among $\dfrac{1}{x}$ persons each performing an amount of work $x < 1$. The result is a total output exceeding unity since $\dfrac{1}{x} \cdot x^m = x^{m-1} > 1$ for $x < 1$, and in fact the finer the division, the greater the total result. This is an empirically unlikely event.

In the following we consider the alternative case $m = 1$ and $m > 1$ constant or increasing returns.

17.2 Larger Output: Simple Organization

Consider now output exceeding unity, i.e., the capacity of one individual. A simple organization is now required. The question is how much time shall be allocated to management.

In small organizations, a person designated as manager, whether permanently or on a rotating basis, may still want to devote part of his/her time to operative labor, say x_{10} leaving time x_{11} for management. But no more than one person may perform management functions in a simple organization. The production function for this type of organization is therefore

$$\phi(x) = \underset{\substack{x_0 + x_{10} + x_{11} \leq x \\ x_{11} \leq 1}}{\text{Max}} \ F(x_0 + x_{10}, x_{11})$$

<u>Proposition 2.</u>

$$\text{Let} \quad 1 = \underset{\substack{x_0, x_1 \\ x_0 + x_1 = 1}}{\text{Max}} \quad F(x_0, x_1) = F(u,v)$$

u,v are the output maximizing allocations of labor to operative work and management in producing a unit output. Then

$$\phi(x) = x^m \qquad \text{for all} \quad x \leqq \frac{1}{v}.$$

<u>Proof.</u> The constraint $x_{11} \leqq 1$ is inoperative as long as $vx \leqq 1$. Therefore, the previous production functions $\phi(x)$ still applies to all $x \leqq \frac{1}{v}$. $\qquad ||$

All larger outputs are produced under the additional constraint $x_{11} = 1$ which implies $x_{10} = 0$.

$$\phi(x) = \underset{\substack{x_0 + x_1 = x \\ x_1 \leqq 1}}{\text{Max}} \quad F(x_0, x_1)$$

$$= \underset{\substack{x_0 + x_1 = x \\ x_1 = 1}}{\text{Max}} \quad F(x_0 x_1)$$

or

$$\phi(x) = F(x-1, 1) \qquad\qquad x \geqq \frac{1}{v}. \qquad\qquad (1)$$

Varying one input (operative labor) while holding the other constant (management) is the classical situation to which the law of diminishing returns to substitution applies. We postulate

<u>Assumption.</u> $F(x_0, x_1)$ for x_1 = constant is a concave function of x_0.

This implies immediately

<u>Proposition 3.</u> $\phi(x)$ is a concave function of x for $x \geq \frac{1}{v}$.

The production function ϕ has, therefore, the following characteristics for $m \geq 1$.

$$\phi(x) = \begin{cases} x^m, & \text{convex} & \text{for} & x < \frac{1}{v} \\ F(x-1,1), & \text{concave} & \text{for} & x \geq \frac{1}{v}. \end{cases} \tag{2}$$

As an illustration, consider a Cobb-Douglas function

$$F(x_0 x_1) = b x_0^{\alpha} x_1^{\beta} \qquad \alpha + \beta = m \geq 1 \tag{3}$$

$$\phi(x) = \max_{x_0 + x_1 = x} b x_0^{\alpha} x_1^{\beta}$$

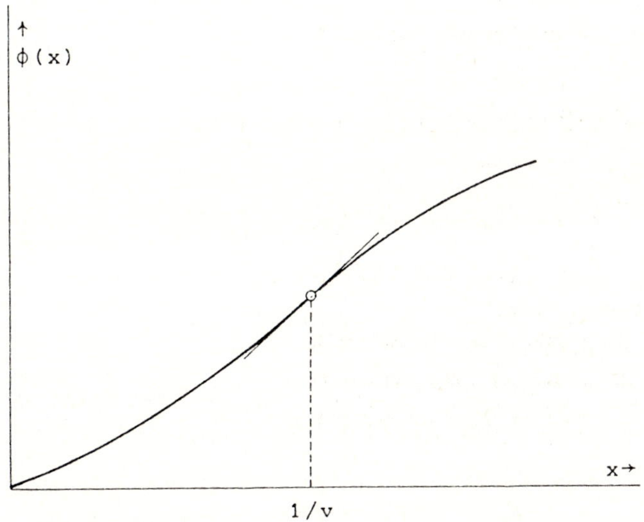

Figure 17.1.   Output of a Simple Organization

implies

$$x_0 = \frac{\alpha}{\alpha+\beta}\, x \qquad\qquad \text{or}\quad u = \frac{\alpha}{\alpha+\beta}$$

$$x_1 = \frac{\beta}{\alpha+\beta}\, x \qquad\qquad\qquad v = \alpha^{\beta}+\beta$$

$$\phi(x) = b\alpha^{\alpha}\,\beta^{\beta}\,(\alpha+\beta)^{-\alpha-\beta}\,x^{\alpha+\beta}.$$

From (2), we have

$$m = \alpha+\beta$$

$$b = \alpha^{-\alpha}\,\beta^{-\beta}(\alpha+\beta)^{\alpha+\beta} \tag{7}$$

$$\phi(x) = \begin{cases} x^{\alpha+\beta} & x \leq \dfrac{\alpha+\beta}{\beta} \\[2ex] (\alpha+\beta)^{\alpha+\beta}\alpha^{-\alpha}\beta^{-\beta}(x-1)^{\alpha} & x \geq \dfrac{\alpha+\beta}{\beta} \end{cases} \tag{8}$$

Observe that $\phi(x)$ is continuously differentiable at $x = \frac{1}{v}$, but that its second derivative is, in general, discontinuous there. This function has been graphed in Figure 17.1 for $\alpha = \frac{3}{4}$ $\beta = \frac{1}{2}$.

With these output elasticities, representing significant returns to scale, one obtains

    a productivity coefficient b = 2.31929
    an optimal span of control s = 9.155
    profits   = 3.0517

These numbers are sensitive to the assumed returns to scale. Thus under milder returns to scale, e.g., $\alpha = \frac{3}{4}$, $\beta = \frac{1}{3}$, $m = 1.08333$ one obtains

$$b = 1.952$$

$$s = 4.59$$

profit $\quad k = 1.530$

17.3 Advantage of Simple Organization

Is organization advantageous? We show:

Proposition 4. Suppose F is homogeneous of degree m. Then the return to organization k exceeds or equals the opportunity wage of unity according as m is greater or equal to one.

$$k \left\{ \begin{matrix} > \\ = \end{matrix} \right\} 1 \quad <==> \quad m \left\{ \begin{matrix} > \\ = \end{matrix} \right\} 1 \tag{1}$$

Proof: A maximum of

$$\phi(x) - (x-1)$$

occurs only where ϕ is concave, hence for $x \geqslant \frac{1}{v}$. Then

$$\phi(x) = F(x-1,1).$$

Now

$$F(x-1,1) = x^m F(\tfrac{x-1}{x}, \tfrac{1}{x})$$

$$= x^m \quad \text{for} \quad x = \frac{1}{v}$$

so that

$$k = \underset{x}{\text{Max}} \quad F(x-1,1) - (x-1) \geqq (\tfrac{1}{v})^m - (\tfrac{1}{v} - 1)$$

$$= 1 + \tfrac{1}{v} (v^{1-m}-1) > 1 \qquad (2)$$

since $v < 1, \quad m > 1.$

If $m = 1$ then

$$\phi(x) \leqq x \qquad \text{and}$$

$$= x \quad \text{for} \quad x \leqq \tfrac{1}{v}$$

from which

$$k = \underset{x}{\text{Max}} \quad \phi(x) - (x-1) = 1 \qquad\qquad (3)$$

We conclude that under constant returns to scale and when operators are paid their full opportunity wage, the reward for organization is just equal to the wage. Therefore, organizations cannot do any better than indivdiuals. There is no economic reason for organization. These conclusions are based on the assumption that operators are paid a unit wage equal to the full opportunity costs of what they could earn on their own.

In some activities operating on one's own is risky. Risk averse operators would, therefore, accept less than a unit wage in exchange for the security of working in an organization. Let this wage be $w < 1$. We recalculate profits of a simple organization when returns to scale are constant.

Without restriction assume that management is full time $x_1 = 1.$

$$\text{Max}_{x_0} \quad f(x_0, 1) - w x_0$$

$$> \text{Max}_{x_0} \quad f(x_0, 1) - x_0 = g(1) \quad \text{for} \quad w < 1.$$

In the Cobb-Douglas case

$$k(w) = \text{Max}_{x_0} \quad b x_0^\alpha - w x_0 \tag{1}$$

is realized when $\alpha b x_0^{\alpha - k} - w = 0$

yielding a span of control

$$s = x_0 = \left(\frac{\alpha b}{w}\right)^{\frac{1}{1-\alpha}} \tag{2}$$

and profits

$$k(w) = (1-\alpha)\left(\frac{\alpha}{w}\right)^{\frac{\alpha}{1-\alpha}} b^{\frac{1}{1-\alpha}} \tag{3}$$

$$= \beta \left(\frac{\alpha}{w}\right)^{\frac{\alpha}{\beta}} b^{\frac{1}{\beta}} \quad \text{in view of} \quad \alpha + \beta = 1.$$

Substituting $b = \alpha^{-\alpha} \beta^{-\beta}$ from (17.2.7)

$$b = -\frac{\alpha}{\beta}$$

$$k(w) = w \tag{4}$$

$$s(w) = \frac{\alpha}{\beta} w^{-\frac{1}{\beta}} \tag{5}$$

For the conventional values $\alpha = \frac{3}{4}$, $\beta = \frac{1}{4}$ Table 17.1 shows profits and spans of control as a function of wages. They turn out to be highly sensitive to the wage rate.

wage rates	w	1	.95	.9	.8	.7	.6	.5
profits	k	0	1.166	1.372	1.953	2.915	4.63	8
span	s	3	3.68	4.57	7.32	12.5	23.1	48

If $m < 1$, the case of diminishing returns to scale, then the return per unit effort

$$\frac{\phi(x)}{x} = x^{m-1} \tag{6}$$

is a decreasing function of x. Hence, the greatest reward is earned by dividing one's work time into the largest possible number n of jobs so that $x = \frac{1}{n}$ is minimized. Only technical considerations will limit x from below and hence bound n from above. Part time work of minimal length does occur in the domestic sphere. This case is of little interest, however, in the study of organizations.

17.4 Utilizing Better Qualified Personnel

So far, all personnel was assumed to be equally qualified both in the operative and the managerial roles. Suppose now that there are two types of persons with qualification q and 1 respectively. These are the quantities of labor in efficiency units possessed by the two types of person. These quantities are assumed to apply both to managerial and operative work. We ask: should better qualified persons ($q > 1$) be assigned to operative or to managerial work?

When used as operatives, the opportunity wage of qualified persons is q. What is their productivity in managerial jobs?

A qualified person used as manager contributes $x_1 = q$. In terms of the production function $F(x_0, x_1)$ with returns to scale of degree m, the surplus obtained by using a qualified person as manager equals

$$
\begin{aligned}
k_q &= \underset{\substack{x_0, x_1 \\ x_1 \le q}}{\text{Max}} \quad F(x_0, x_1) - x_0 \\[2em]
&= \underset{\substack{x_0, x_1 \\ x_1 \le q}}{\text{Max}} \quad q^m \left(F\left(\frac{x_0}{q}, \frac{x_1}{q}\right) \right) - x_0 \\[2em]
&= \underset{\substack{z_0, z_1 \\ z_1 \le 1}}{\text{Max}} \quad q^m F(z_0, z_1) - q \cdot z_0 \\[2em]
&> q \; \underset{\substack{z_0, z_1 \\ z_0 \le 1}}{\text{Max}} \quad [F(z_0, z_1) - z_0] \\[2em]
&= q \cdot k
\end{aligned}
$$

by definition (14.9) of k.
This proves that a person of qualification q (in efficiency units) makes his/her largest contribution $k_q > q \cdot k > q$ as manager. The ablest should rise to the top.

18 Management Motivation: Principal and Agent

<u>18.1 Introduction</u>

From the economic perspective, what drives the advance of organizations are the profits to be made by founding a simple organization to take over functions previously performed by individuals. What if the founder and owner turns over the management to a hired manager? What incentives does such a hired manager have to achieve the organization's goals? Specifically for profit-making organizations, how should the manager be rewarded to motivate him/her towards the achievement of maximum net profits for the owner?

This is an example of the well-known "principal-agent" paradigm (Stiglitz, 1974). To set it in context we must specify the information available to principal and agent. We shall consider the simplest scenario: The owner(s) are heirs of the founder and have no knowledge of the business. In particular they cannot judge how much effort x_1 the hired manager actually puts into the running of the (simple) organization. Moreover, the manager is free to choose the number of operatives x_0. To begin with it is not even clear that the manager will supervise the operatives sufficiently so as to achieve the output

$$F(x_0, x_1)$$

attainable with the inputs into the production function F. We assume that the manager knows the production function, but the owners do not. Among the possible compensations schemes we consider only one: The manager receives a fixed proportion δ of the gross profits. The question is then to choose δ so as to maximize the owner's net profits.

Since the manager now has a direct interest in the organization's profits, he/she will indeed seek maximum output from given inputs, as described by the production function.

18.2 Managers as Principals

We begin by modelling a production function for the organization's output. Suppose that the main task of management is to monitor the performance of operatives. An operative is expected to work full time $t = 1$ but may choose to shirk, be idle, part of the time. Let an operative's utility function be

$$u = h \ln (2-t) + y \tag{1}$$

where u   utility

  y   income

  $h > 0$ a parameter measuring the attractiveness of leisure.

When $t < 1$ the operative is idle for the fraction $1 - t$ of working time. If q is the probability of being caught and k the penalty imposed in the form of lost wages or reprimands then the objective of an operative should be to maximize his/her utility in terms of leisure and penalties

$$\max_{0 \leq t \leq 1} \ h \ln (2-t) + q(1-t) \cdot (-k)$$

A solution $t < 1$ exists if

$$- \frac{h}{2-t} + qk = 0$$

$$t = 2 - \frac{h}{k} \ \frac{1}{q} < 1 \tag{2}$$

Now q is the proportion of time that x_1 supervisors allocate to the x_0 operatives. If this allocation is random, then the probability w of being caught shirking is

$$q = \frac{x_1}{x_0}$$

yielding

$$t = 2 - \frac{h}{k}\,\frac{x_0}{x_1} \qquad (3)$$

This is the supply function of individual labor. To fix the parameter h consider how much a person would work voluntarily for a unit reward per unit time when on his/her own

$$\underset{t}{\text{Max}} \quad h \ln (2-t) + t$$

This is solved by

$$-\frac{h}{2-t} + 1 = 0$$

or

$$t = 2 - h$$

If this working time is assumed to be unity then

$$h = 1.$$

Substituting in (3)

$$t = 2 - \frac{1}{k}\,\frac{x_0}{x_1} \qquad (4)$$

Equation (3) shows that there is a maximum ratio of operatives to managers or span of control $\dfrac{x_0}{x_1}$ that involves sufficient supervision per operative to guarantee full-time work $t = 1$.

$$\frac{x_0}{x_1} \leq \frac{k}{h} \qquad (5)$$

This span of control equals the penalty for shirking divided by the coefficient of the preference for leisure.

Up to this critical control span the output of the organization, which we assumed to be proportional to labor input, is also proportional to the number of operatives

$$y = bx_0 \quad \text{for} \quad \frac{x_0}{x_1} \leqslant \frac{k}{h} \tag{6a}$$

When the control span is larger, then (4) applies so that

$$y = bx_1 \left(2 - \frac{h}{k}\frac{x_0}{x_1}\right) \quad \text{for} \quad \frac{x_0}{x_1} \geqslant \frac{k}{h} \tag{6b}$$

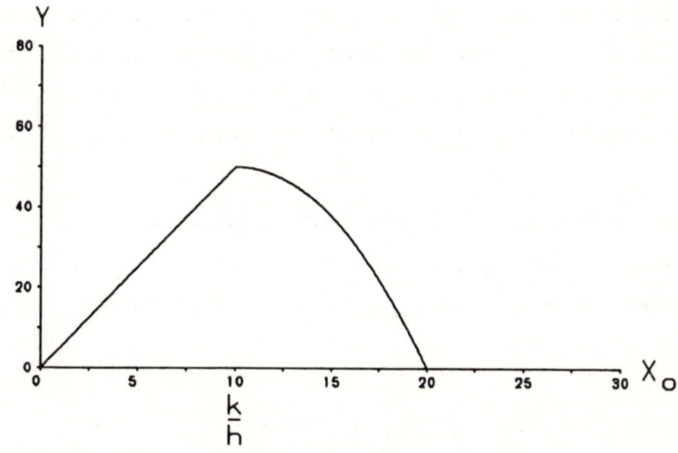

Figure 18.1. Output of Monitored Operatives when $x_1 = 1$

The production function (6a), (6b) is shown in Figure   .

Profits $y - x_0$ are maximal when the control span is at its critical level, for

$$\frac{d}{dx_0}(y - x_0) = 2 - \frac{2h}{k}\frac{x_0}{x_1} = 0$$

implies

$$\frac{x_0}{x_1} = \frac{k}{h} \tag{5a}$$

Achieved profits are then

$$G = (b-1)x_0$$

$$= (b-1)\,\frac{k}{h}\,x_1 \qquad\qquad \text{using (5a)}.$$

Profit is thus proportional to managerial effort x_1.

The combination of managerial and operative inputs in an organization need not take the specific form described so far. It will, however, be subject to some type of production function $F(x_0, x_1)$ describing the maximal output an organization can achieve when a manager puts in x_1 time units of effort and the operatives supply x_0 time unit of effort (see Chapters 12-16).

18.3 Linear Homogeneous Production Function

That profit is proportional to managerial effort x_1 is true for all linear homogeneous production functions. This may be seen as follows:

$$G(x_1) = \underset{x_0}{\text{Max}}\ \{F(x_0, x_1) - x_0\}$$

$$= x_1\ \underset{x_0}{\text{Max}}\ \{F(\frac{x_0}{x_1}) - \frac{x_0}{x_1}\}$$

$$= x_1\ \underset{u}{\text{Max}}\ \{F(u) - u\}$$

$$= x_1 \cdot g_1 \qquad\qquad (\text{say}) \tag{1}$$

As an example we may consider the linear homogeneous Cobb-Douglas function.

$$y = bx_0^{\alpha} x_1^{\beta} \qquad \alpha = \frac{3}{4} \qquad \beta = \frac{1}{4} \qquad (2)$$

With this Cobb-Douglas production function profits as a function of managerial effort are

$$G(x_1) = \underset{x_0}{\text{Max}} \ \{bx_0^{\alpha} x_1^{\beta} - x_0\}$$

$$= x_1 \ \text{Max} \ \{b(\frac{x_0}{x_1})^{\alpha} - \frac{x_0}{x_1}\}$$

$$= x_1 \ \text{Max} \ \{bu^{\alpha} - u\}$$

$$= x_1 \cdot g_1$$

where g_1 is determined by

$$0 = \alpha bu^{\alpha-1} - 1$$

$$u = (\alpha b)^{\frac{1}{1-\alpha}}$$

$$g_1 = b(\alpha b)^{\frac{\alpha}{1-\alpha}} - (\alpha b)^{\frac{1}{1-\alpha}}$$

$$g_1 = (1-\alpha) \ b^{\frac{1}{1-\alpha}} \alpha^{\frac{\alpha}{1-\alpha}} \qquad (3)$$

To determine b assume that the product or service produced by the organization can also be supplied by an individual operating on his/her own under the same production function.

If a single person allocates his/her time among management and operative labor

$$x_0 + x_1 = 1$$

then an optimal allocation of effort requires

$$\frac{\partial y}{\partial x_0} = \frac{\partial y}{\partial x_1}$$

or

$$\frac{\alpha y}{x_0} = \frac{\beta y}{x_1} \qquad \frac{x_0}{x_1} = \frac{\alpha}{\beta} \qquad\qquad \text{from which}$$

$$x_0 = \alpha \qquad x_1 = \beta \qquad\qquad \text{so that}$$

$$1 = b\alpha^{\alpha}\beta^{\beta} \qquad\qquad \text{implying}$$

$$b = \alpha^{-\alpha}\beta^{-\beta}$$

But if an independent individual earns 50% more than a hired operative, then

$$1.5 = b\alpha^{\alpha}\,\beta^{\beta} \qquad\qquad \text{or}$$

$$b = 1.5\,\left(\tfrac{3}{4}\right)^{-\frac{3}{4}}\left(\tfrac{1}{4}\right)^{-\frac{1}{4}} = 2.6177778$$

Substituting this b in (9) yields

$$g_1 = \tfrac{1}{4}\,(2.6178)^4 \cdot \left(\tfrac{3}{4}\right)^3$$

$$= 4.955$$

The "marginal productivity" g_1 of a manager is thus almost five times that of an operative (whose marginal productivity is 1).

18.4 Managers as Agents

Next we determine the level of effort chosen by the manager as a function of his/her rewards. The reward may take any form: a fixed salary w_1 or a share δ of total profits g are two possibilities. Between these extremes may be found other types of compensation usually consisting of some fixed payment and some bonus that is proportional to achieved profits.

Here we shall consider that a manager receives only a share δ of total profits G. When the production function is linear homogeneous this reward turns out to be proportional to managerial effort

$$\delta g = \delta g_1 \cdot x_1$$

To determine the manager's voluntary effort one must consider his/her utility function in terms of leisure $2 - x_1$, and money income $\delta g_1 x_1$.

Effort is measured in time units and total available time is two units. As before let utility be additive, logarithmic in terms of leisure, and linear in terms of income.

$$u = h \ln (2-x_1) + \delta g x_1 \tag{1}$$

The factor h measures the attractiveness of leisure in relation to that of income and may differ among individuals and between operatives. A utility maximizing manager chooses an effort level x_1 such that

$$0 = \frac{du}{dx_1} = \frac{-h}{2-x_1} + \delta g$$

from which

$$x_1 = 2 - \frac{h}{\delta g} \qquad (2)$$

This is an increasing function of share δ and may be considered the manager's supply function of effort (Figure).

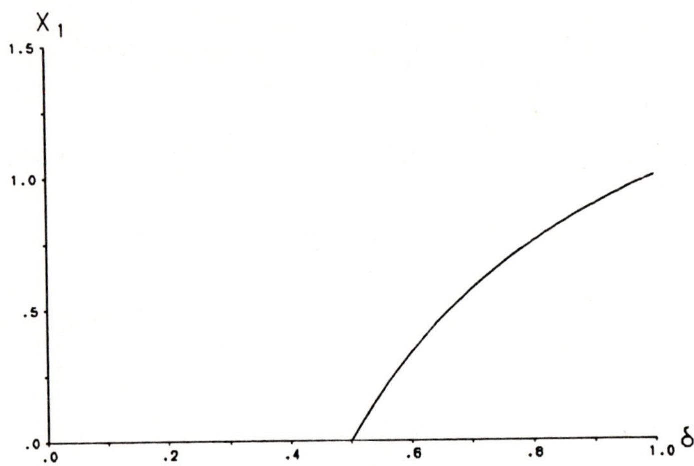

Figure 18.2. Manager's Effort as a Function of Profit Share

The manager's achieved income is then

$$\delta/x_1 = 2\delta g_1 - h$$

This is positive provided the profitability g_1 of the organization and the manager's share δ are large enough relative to the strength h of the preference for leisure. When $h = 1$ (normal preference for leisure) then the manager's income exceeds that of a worker $w_0 = 1$ provided the profit share δg exceeds unity.

Consider now the owner's income. It is

$$z = (1-\delta)g_1$$

or in view of (7), (11)

$$z = (1-\delta)g_1 x_1 = 2(1-\delta) - \frac{h(1-\delta)}{\delta} \tag{3}$$

Maximization of owner's income with respect to the manager's share δ yields

$$0 = \frac{\partial z}{\partial \delta} = -2g_1 - \frac{-h\delta - h(1-\delta)}{\delta^2}$$

$$0 = -2g_1 + \frac{h}{\delta^2} \quad \text{or}$$

$$\delta = \sqrt{\frac{h}{2g_1}} \tag{4}$$

Using (13), the manager's rate of reward, i.e., his/her portion of unit profits per unit effort becomes

$$\delta g = \sqrt{\frac{h}{2}}\, g_1 \tag{5}$$

This is reminiscent of von Thünen's famous wage formula: An employee's compensation is to be set proportional to the square root of his/her productivity g_1. ($\frac{h}{2}$ would have to represent subsistence income for a full analogy.)

Suppose that for this reward a manager puts in a full-time effort $x_1 = 1$. Using (11) this means that

$$1 = 2 - \frac{h}{\delta g} = 2 - \frac{h}{\delta\sqrt{\frac{h}{2g}}}$$

Necessary and sufficient for this is that $h = \frac{g}{2}$.

Substitution in (18.3.3) yields

$$\delta = \frac{1}{2}$$

the time honored half share in share cropping. While this is valid for all linear homogeneous production functions, it does depend on the specific utility function and its parameters.

So far, we considered simple organizations, requiring only one managerial level. In multi-level organizations an agency problem could arise at every level. Suppose, however, that it is only top management--the president--who can freely choose his level of managerial effort, while all lower ranking managers are fully supervised and require no additional incentive. Now the managerial mode of "management by delegation" implies in fact constant returns to scale, i.e., a linear homogeneous production function for the entire organization (Ch. 19 infra). The previous analysis is thus applicable to the compensation of top management in hierarchical organizations.

18.5 Increasing Returns to Scale

In simple organizations we may have increasing returns to scale. Let $F(x_0, x_1)$ be homogeneous of degree $m > 1$ and Cobb-Douglas. Now, for given x_1

$$g(x_1) = \underset{x_0}{\text{Max}} \quad bx_0^{\alpha} x_1^{\beta} - x_0 \tag{16}$$

is achieved for $\alpha bx_0^{\alpha-1} x_1^{\beta} = 1$

or $\qquad x_0 = (\alpha bx_1^{\beta})^{\frac{1}{1-\alpha}}$

Substituting in (16) yields

$$g(x_1) = (1-\alpha) \; \alpha^{\frac{\alpha}{1-\alpha}} \; b^{\frac{1}{1-\alpha}} \; x_1^{\frac{\beta}{1-\alpha}}$$

$$g(x_1) = g_1 \cdot x_1^{\frac{\beta}{1-\alpha}} \tag{17}$$

Notice that

$$\frac{\beta}{1-\alpha} > 1$$

in view of $\quad m = \alpha + \beta > 1$

The manager's earnings as a function of effort x_1 are

$$\delta \cdot g \cdot x_1^{\frac{\beta}{1-\alpha}} \tag{18}$$

and his/her utility function is

$$y = h \ln (2-x_1) + \delta g \cdot x_1^{\frac{\beta}{1-\alpha}}$$

This is maximized with respect to effort x_1 when

$$0 = -\frac{h}{2-x_1} + \delta g \; \frac{\beta}{1-\alpha} \cdot x_1^{\frac{\alpha+\beta-1}{1-\alpha}}$$

or

$$(2-x_1) x_1^{\frac{\alpha+\beta-1}{1-\alpha}} = \frac{h(1-\alpha)}{\delta g \beta} \tag{19}$$

Suppose for instance that

$$\alpha = \frac{3}{4} \qquad \beta = \frac{1}{2}$$

then (19) becomes

$$(2-x_1)x_1 = a \tag{20}$$

where

$$a = \frac{1}{2\delta} \cdot \frac{h}{g}$$

Equation (20) is solved by

$$x_1 = 1 + \sqrt{1-a}$$

Profits achieved are then

$$y = g \cdot x_1^2$$

$$= g \cdot \{1 + \sqrt{1-a}\}^2 \tag{21}$$

The owner's earnings are then

$$z = (1-\delta)y$$

$$z = (1-\delta) \left\{1 + \frac{1}{2\delta} \frac{h}{g}\right\}^2$$

Maximizing z with respect to δ yields

$$\delta = \frac{1}{2} \frac{h}{g} \tag{22}$$

This implies, using (20), $a = 1$ and

$$x_1 = 1$$

The manager puts in a full-time effort resulting in profits

$$y = g$$

The principal's return is then

$$z = (1 - \frac{1}{2} \frac{h}{g}) g$$

$$z = g - \frac{h}{2}$$

and the manager's reward δg equals

$$w_1 = \frac{h}{2}$$

Notice that this is proportional to the strength h of his preference for leisure. The manager's utility is then

$$u = \frac{h}{2}$$

This exceeds the utility achieved by an operative with unit wage only when $h > 2$.

In particular when

$$h = g$$

then principal and agent once more divide profits equally

$$z = w_1 = \frac{g}{2}$$

On the other hand, when $h = \frac{g}{2}$ as assumed in the linear homogeneous case, then

$$\delta = \frac{1}{4}$$

It appears from this that increasing returns to scale are beneficial to the principal.

19 The Economics of Hierarchy

We now turn to the question raised in the beginning of this chapter: If organization is advantageous at the simple level $R = 1$, what, if any, are the economic advantages of hierarchical organizations with more than one level of supervision, $R > 1$?

19.1 Management by Delegation

At the outset it is useful to distinguish between two styles of management: Management by team work and management by delegation. The first combines the inputs of $x_1 = 1$ supervisor with $x_0 = x$ subordinates in a joint effort. It is described by the production function

$$F(x_0, x_1) = F(1, x)$$

and is assumed to be the applicable type in simple organizations.

In management by delegation each person acts on his/her own with a certain amount of supervision by his/her supervisor. In terms of the production function we have

$$x \quad \text{individuals producing} \quad F(1, \tfrac{1}{x})$$

for a total of

$$x \, F(1, \tfrac{1}{x}).$$

This will be written

$$f(x, 1) \equiv xF(1, \tfrac{1}{x}) \qquad \text{or more generally}$$

$$f(x_0, x_1) \equiv x_0 F(1, \tfrac{x_1}{x_0})$$

By construction $f(x_0, x_1)$ is linear homogeneous. The reader
should verify that

$$f(\lambda x_0, \lambda x_1) = \lambda f(x_0, x_1)$$

Define now

$$h = \underset{x}{\text{Max}} \quad xF(1, \tfrac{1}{x}) - x = h \tag{1}$$

Then

$$m < h < k.$$

<u>Proof</u>: To show the right inequality observe that

$$x\, F(x, \tfrac{1}{x}) = x^{1-m}\, F(x,1) \tag{2}$$

by homogeneity of F

$$< F(x,1) \quad \text{for} \quad x > 1 \quad m > 1$$

(Recall that the maximizing x is not less than $\tfrac{1}{v} > 1$.)
To prove the left-hand inequality write

$$x\, F(1, \tfrac{1}{x}) - x = x(1 + \tfrac{1}{x})^m\, F\left(\frac{1}{1 + \tfrac{1}{x}}, \frac{1/x}{1 + \tfrac{1}{x}}\right) - x \tag{3}$$

Now $\qquad F\left(\dfrac{1}{1 + \tfrac{1}{x}}, \dfrac{1/x}{1 + \tfrac{1}{x}}\right) = 1$

for $\dfrac{1}{x+1} = v$ or $x = \dfrac{1}{v} - 1 = \hat{x}$ (say). Substituting in (3)

$$= \hat{x}\left[(1 + \tfrac{1}{\hat{x}})^m - 1\right]$$

$$\geq \hat{x}[1 + \frac{m}{\hat{x}} - 1] = m \quad \text{using a Taylor expansion.}$$

Therefore

$$h = \underset{x}{\text{Max}} \; x \, F(1, \frac{1}{x}) - x > m. \quad \| \|$$

We have thus shown that m is a lower bound to k as well.

Example: Consider the Cobb-Douglas case

$$F(x_0, x_1) = (\alpha+\beta)^{\alpha+\beta} \; \alpha^{-\alpha} \; \beta^{-\beta} \; x_0^{\alpha} \; x_1^{\beta}$$

$$= m^m \; (m-\beta)^{\beta-m} \; \beta^{-\beta} \; x_0^{\alpha} \; x_1^{\beta}$$

$$f(x,1) = x \, F(1, \frac{1}{x})$$

$$= m^m \; (m-\beta)^{\beta-m} \; \beta^{-\beta} \; x^{1-\beta}$$

Then

$$\underset{x}{\text{Max}} \quad f(x,1) - x \quad \text{yields}$$

$$h = m^{\frac{m}{\beta}} \; (m-\beta)^{\frac{\beta-m}{m}} \; (1-\beta)^{\frac{1-\beta}{\beta}}$$

it may be shown (by L'Hopital's rule) that $h = m$ for $\beta = 0$ and h is an increasing function of β.

19.2 Optimization

Our principal result is the following:

Theorem:

$$f(x_0, f(x_1, \ldots, f(x_{R-1}1) \ldots)) \leq x_0 + hx_1 + \ldots$$

$$+ h^{R-1} x_{R-1} + h^R \qquad (4)$$

and "=" if and only if

$$x_r = \sigma(\sigma+h)^{R-r-1} \qquad r = 0, \ldots, R-1.$$

Here σ denotes the maximizer of $f(x,1) - x$. This theorem
will be called "The Theorem on Returns to Scale in Nested
Organizational Production Function" for reasons explained below.
The proof will be given for $R = 3$. Consider

$$f(x_0, f(x_1, f(x_2,1))) \leqq f(x_0, f(x_1, h + x_2))$$

using (1);

$$= (h+x_2) \, f(\frac{x_0}{h+x_2}, \, f(\frac{x_1}{h+x_2}), \, 1))$$

using linear homogeneity of f;

$$\leqq (h+x_2) \, f(\frac{x_0}{h+x_2}, \, h + \frac{x_1}{h+x_2})$$

using (1);

$$= (h+x_2)(h + \frac{x_1}{h+x_2}) \cdot f(\frac{\dfrac{x_0}{h+x_2}}{h + \dfrac{x_1}{h+x_2}}, \, 1)$$

using linear homogeneity;

$$\leqq (h+x_2)(h + \frac{x_1}{h+x_2})(h + \frac{\dfrac{x_0}{h+x_2}}{h + \dfrac{x_1}{h+x_2}})$$

using (1);

$$= h^3 + h^2 x_2 + hx_1 + x_0$$

The "=" is taken on when

$$x_2 = \sigma$$

$$\frac{x_1}{h+x_2} = \sigma \qquad (5)$$

$$\frac{\dfrac{x_0}{h+x_2}}{h + \dfrac{x_1}{h+x_2}} = \sigma$$

The first two equations imply

$$x_1 = (h+\sigma)\sigma \qquad (6)$$

Substituting in the last equation one has

$$x_0 = (h+\sigma)^2 \sigma. \qquad || \qquad (7)$$

19.3 Discussion: Emerging Wage Structure

This theorem can be interpreted as follows.

If a simple organization is advantageous and achieves the payoff h^* with team management and h using management by delegation, then a multi-level organization is advantageous provided employees of rank r receive an opportunity wage h^r. The organization's profit or presidential payment is then h^R. Thus organizational advantage is escalated through the application of successive levels of management, but not at the rate k for team work, but at the lower rate h for management by delegation.

We conclude: Whether a particular activity or industry is carried out in multi-level organizations rather than by simple organizations depends on the size of h relative to k. If h

is sufficiently close to k when managers are willing to accept
this as compensation rather than the full opportunity wage k
that one might achieve on one's own. Of course, running a simple
organization of one's own requires team work as well as various
other things such as initiative, access to capital, etc., in other
words, entrepreneurship rather than just managerial capability.
If h is too small, then the activity is one for which only
simple organizations will be found advantageous.

In addition, there will be activities where not even simple
organizations are practical since $k \leq 1$. At present there are
only a few of these left, and these are found mainly in the fields
of art and writing.

That managers receive a higher wage than operatives is
consistent with long-run equilibrium and free entry provided we
assume managerial talent to be limited and/or the effort level in
management to exceed that required in operative work.

19.4 <u>Loss of Control</u>

Consider now the possibility of control loss at a rate
$\rho \leq 1$. By definition the president's control is effective

$$y_R = x_R$$

but managerial control y_r at all levels $r < R$ is now reduced
to

$$\rho y_r .$$

The managerial production function is then transformed to

$$\frac{y_r}{k_r} = \rho F(1, \frac{y_{r+1}}{x_r})$$

Substituting in the organizational production function

$$Q = f(x_0, \rho f(x_1, \ldots, \rho f(x_{R-1}, 1) \ldots))$$

The theorem on scale returns in nested production functions must now be modified as follows.

$$Q \leqq \rho^{R-1} h^R + \rho^{R-1} h^{R-1} x_{R-1} + \ldots + \rho h x_1 + x_0 \qquad (1)$$

and

$$\text{"="} \quad \text{if} \quad x_r = \sigma [\rho^r (h+\sigma)]^{R-1-r}$$

The proof follows along the lines of the theorem and is left to the reader.

We interpret this result as follows. Loss of control can be corrected and compensated by making the following adjustments:

the rate of managerial pay is reduced from h^r to $(\rho h)^r$

the president's compensation is reduced to

$$\rho^{R-1} h^R;$$

the span of control is reduced to

$$\rho(h+\sigma) \quad \text{for} \quad r = 1, \ldots, R-1$$

and is left unchanged for the president.

In fact, consider the total output under these conditions. Using (8)

$$Q = \rho^{R-1}h^R + \rho^{R-1}h^{R-1}\sigma + \rho^{R-2}h^{R-2}\rho\sigma(\sigma+h)$$

$$+ \ldots + \sigma\rho^{R-1}(\sigma+h)^{R-1}$$

$$= \rho^{R-1}h^R + \rho^{R-1}\sigma h^{R-1}[1 + \frac{\sigma+h}{h} + \ldots (\frac{\sigma+h}{h})^{R-1}]$$

$$= \rho^{R-1}h^R + \sigma(\rho h)^{R-1} \frac{(\frac{\sigma+h}{h})^R - 1}{\frac{\sigma+h}{h} - 1}$$

$$= \rho^{R-1}h^R + \rho^{R-1}h^R[(\frac{\sigma+h}{h})^R - 1]$$

$$Q = \rho^{R-1}(\sigma+h)^R \tag{2}$$

The total number of operatives is

$$n_0 = \sigma\rho^{R-1}(\sigma+h)^{R-1} \tag{3}$$

Per capita output of operatives is therefore

$$\frac{Q}{n_0} = \frac{\sigma+h}{\sigma} = \frac{1}{1 + \frac{h}{\sigma}} \tag{4}$$

and this is independent of scale R and the control loss factor ρ. Therefore, with the appropriate adjustments of wages and spans of control, per capita output of workers is stabilized at a constant level. The organization operates with constant returns to scale.

Consider also total cost

$$W = \rho^{R-1} h^R + \sum_{r=0}^{R-1} h^r \rho^r \sigma [(\sigma+h)\rho]^{R-r-1}$$

$$= \rho^{R-1} h^R + \rho^{R-1} \sigma (\sigma+h)^{R-1} \sum_{r=0}^{R-1} (\frac{h}{\sigma+h})^r$$

$$= \rho^{R-1} h^R + \rho^{R-1} \sigma (\sigma+h)^{R-1} \frac{1 - (\frac{h}{\sigma+h})^R}{1 - \frac{h}{\sigma+h}}$$

$$= \rho^{R-1} h^R + \rho^{R-1} (\sigma+h)^R - \rho^{R-1} h^R$$

$$= \rho^{R-1} (\sigma+h)^R$$

and this is equal to total output (9).

Cost per unit output is, therefore, unity at all levels of organization and for individual effort. This is but another aspect of constant returns to scale. The surplus achieved through organization is paid out as wage to managers and presidential compensation.

19.5 Team Work at the Top

In an alternative specification the heart of productive effort is assumed to reside in the president and his/her team. Their combined output is described by the original production function applicable to team work

$$F(x_{R-1}, 1)$$

The organizational production function is then modified to

$$Q = f(x_0, \rho f(x_1, \ldots, \rho f(x_{R-2}, F(x_{R-1}, 1) \ldots))$$

Applying the same argument as before one has

$$0 \leqq \rho f(x_{R-2}, k + x_{R-1})$$

$$= (k + x_{R-1}) \, f(\frac{x_0}{k+x_{R-1}}, \; \rho f(\frac{x_1}{k+x_{R-1}}, \; \ldots))$$

from which eventually

$$Q \leqq k(\rho h)^{R-1} + (\rho h)^{R-1} x_{R-1} + \ldots + \rho h x_1 + x_0$$

$$= \quad \text{when} \quad x_r = s \cdot \rho (\sigma + h)^{R-r-1}$$

and s is the maximizer of

$$F(x,1) - x.$$

Here the president is rewarded by an exceptional salary increment

$$k > h,$$

which is due to top level team work. In fact, k is the return
to a simple organization operating as a team.

19.6 Long Run

In the long run the possibility of changes in output price
p and wage w must be considered. We shall use a labor standard
of value and hence keep the wage rate at unity, $w = 1$. Initially
in equilibrium this was also the output price. The coefficients
of the production function must then be such that

$$w = \max_{x_0 + x_1 = 1} pF(x_0, x_1)$$

or in view of $w = 1 \quad p = 1$

$$1 = \underset{x_0 + x_1 = 1}{\text{Max}} \ F(x_0, x_1)$$

Thus in the case of Cobb-Douglas production function it was shown in Section 15 that

$$1 = \underset{x_0 + x_1 = 1}{\text{Max}} \ bx_0^{\alpha} x_1^{\beta}$$

implies

$$b = (\alpha + \beta)^{\alpha + \beta} \ \alpha^{-\alpha} \ \beta^{-\beta}$$

Assume that initially the management technology had constant returns of scale. There is then no incentive to organization since

$$k = \underset{x}{\text{Max}} \ F(x, 1) - x = 1$$

so that an entrepreneur can earn no more than the opportunity wage of unity.

Suppose now that technical change generates a new production function with increasing returns to scale such that the production function is now homogeneous of degree $m > 1$. In the Cobb-Douglas case this means changes in α and/or β, but possibly also in the productivity coefficient a. Suppose now that

$$k = \underset{x}{\text{Max}} \ pF(x, 1) - x > 1 \quad p = 1$$

is sufficiently large to attract organizers $k \geqq k_0$. Then as a result of the increased supply, price p will fall. We show by an example that this price fall may drive out individual operators. This activity is then taken over by simple organizations.

Consider the Cobb-Douglas production function

$$y = bx_0^{\frac{3}{4}} x_1^{\frac{1}{2}}$$

An individual operator's earnings will be

$$w = \operatorname*{Max}_{x_0 + x_1 = 1} pbx_0^{\frac{3}{4}} x_1^{\frac{1}{2}}$$

These earnings are maximized when

$$\frac{x_0}{x_1} = \frac{3}{2} \qquad \frac{\frac{3/4}{x_1}}{} = \frac{\frac{1/2}{x_1}}{} \qquad \text{or} \quad x_0 = \frac{3}{5} \quad x_1 = \frac{2}{5}$$

yielding

$$w = pb(\frac{3}{5})^{\frac{3}{4}} \cdot (\frac{2}{5})^{\frac{1}{2}}$$

$$= pb \; 0.5428$$

The boss of a simple organization earns

$$k = \operatorname*{Max}_{x} pb \; x^{\frac{3}{4}} - x$$

and this is achieved when

$$x = (\tfrac{3}{4}\, pb)^4$$

yielding

$$k = \tfrac{1}{4}\, (pb)^4 \, (\tfrac{3}{4})^3 - \tfrac{29}{256}\, (pb)^4$$

Now

$$w < 1 < k \tag{1}$$

for all   pb   from

$$1.807 < pb < 1.844$$

In particular pb = 1.84 yields k = 1.2089.
The condition for (1) to hold with a Cobb-Douglas function is

$$pb \, (\tfrac{\alpha}{\alpha+\beta})^\alpha (\tfrac{\beta}{\alpha+\beta})^\beta < 1 < (pb)^{\frac{1}{1-\alpha}} \, \alpha^{\frac{\alpha}{1-\alpha}} \, (1-\alpha) \tag{2}$$

This is satisfied whenever

$$\alpha^{-\alpha}(1-\alpha)^{-(1-\alpha)} < pb < (\alpha+\beta)^{\alpha+\beta} \, \alpha^{-\alpha} \, \beta^{-\beta} \tag{3}$$

Now it can be shown that the left-hand expression in (3) is
strictly less than the right-hand expression for all

$$\alpha+\beta \geq 1, \quad \alpha \geq 0, \quad \beta \geq 0$$

in fact

$$\ln\,[(\alpha+\beta)^{\alpha+\beta}]\,-\,\ln\,[\alpha^{-\alpha}(1-\alpha)^{-(1-\alpha)}]\,=\,0$$

for $\quad\alpha+\beta\,=\,1$

and this is an increasing function of α or β.

Therefore, the possibility of organization driving out individuals always exists in a Cobb-Douglas technology with increasing returns.

On the other hand, since

$$k\,>\,h \qquad\qquad\qquad (4)$$

simple organizations will always yield a better return than can be earned by first line managers in a hierarchical organization.

Now first line managers must accept lower rates of pay than individual entrepreneurs. In fact, they may be satisfied with a given h_0 when entrepreneurs are dissatisfied with a larger k_0, $k_0 > h_0$.

Except for this possibility (which according to Frank Knight is unlikely), simple organizations can never be driven out of business by hierarchies. Even the automotive industry has many small firms specializing in various aspects of automobile production, modification and repair, while leaving mass production to hierarchical organizations.

When $m > 1$ but $\rho h < h_0$ is too small, then only simple organizations plus possibly individuals will survive in this activity.

19.7 Organizational Modes of an Industry

To summarize we have the following possibilities:

1) $m < 1$		only part-time activity
2) $m = 1$	$w < 1$	individuals and organizations
3) $m = 1$		individuals only
4) $m > 1$	$1 < h < h_0$	rewards for organization too small and rewards for managers too small; individuals only
5) $m > 1$	$k < k_0$, $\rho h > h_0$	rewards for simple organizations too small but adequate for managers: hierarchies only
6) $m > 1$	$k > k_0$, $\rho h < h_0$	rewards adequate for simple organizations, but not hierarchies
7) $m > 1$	$k > k_0$, $\rho h > h_0$	both hierarchies and simple organizations, no individuals

In cases 5) and 6) individuals may also compete unless simple organizations or hierarchies drive prices below their acceptance level. We conclude with the following remark: The advantage of organization discussed here must be seen against a background of a competitive market economy, in which organizations appear as price takers. The question of economic efficiency changes its nature entirely when organizations become large enough to act as monopolists or as agents of central planning. So does the role of individuals in organizations. By the nature of the control process, freedom of action is restricted in organizations. The only effective protection against enslavement by organizations is their competition for personnel is competitive labor markets.

Seen from this broader perspective, organizations are not only a source of inequality--of results, not necessarily of opportunities--they are also a potential threat to individual liberty. To enjoy a maximum of freedom, one must either be an independent individual operating on one's own (but possibly at an economic sacrifice) or must succeed in reaching the top position in an organization. However, "many are called, but few are chosen."

20 Alternatives to Hierarchy: Partnerships

20.1 <u>Partnership Defined</u>

Supervision implies rank and hierarchy. Hierarchy implies special privileges for the top level, including the possibility of appropriating any surplus. But is hierarchy inevitable?

The privileged position of the top person may be leveled by distributing profits more equitably among organization members. Moreover, the rigor of hierarchy may be reduced by rotating management functions, particularly in a simple organization.

This is the intention of alternative organizations in which the rigors of hierachy give way to the more egalitarian organizational forms of commune or partnership. We shall examine only the latter form, which has after all proved capable of survival in the long run. A partnership is an organization which
. rotates or delegates supervision
. shares profits among all partners according to some specified rule.

In this chapter we compare the operations of a partnership to those of a simple proprietary organization.

What is its optimal size?

What are its maximal profits?

When is partnership preferred to individual operation or to ownership of a simple organization?

For a partnership to be preferred to individual operation, the same condition must be fulfilled as for a proprietorship to be profitable, i.e., increasing returns to scale. The case when profits result from paying less than the opportunity wage does not apply here. Thus partnerships are not attractive under constant returns to scale, except possibly as a device for reducing risk. (But considerations of risk are left out of this monograph.)

Throughout this chapter, we therefore assume increasing returns to scale, or more specifically, a production function in terms of operative work x_0 and management $x_1 \leqslant 1$ which is homogeneous of degree $m > 1$.

20.2 Equal Sharing and Full Time Work

To get our bearings consider first a partnership in which each person contributes one unit (i.e., full time) of effort and receives an equal share of total profits as sole reward. What is the optimal size of such a partnership and how does a partner's income compare to that of a proprietor?

As shown in Chapter 17, increasing returns imply that management should be full time $x_1 = 1$. With x partners and equal sharing, a partner's income is

$$g = \frac{F(x-1,1)}{x}.$$

The optimal number of partners is that which maximizes each partner's income

$$g = \operatorname*{Max}_{x} \ \frac{F(x-1,1)}{x} \tag{1}$$

Suppose that the optimum allocation of an individual's effort to operative work and management is u,v where $u + v = 1$ (cf. Section 17.1) so that

$$F(u,v) = 1$$

let

$$x = \frac{1}{v} > 1.$$

Then

$$1 = F(\frac{x-1}{x}, \frac{1}{x})$$

$$x^m = x^m F(\frac{x-1}{x}, \frac{1}{x}) = F(x-1,1) \tag{2}$$

so that

$$F(x-1,1) > x \quad \text{whenever} \quad m > 1. \tag{3}$$

Increasing returns to scale will thus create a partner's income above the unit wage

$$g > 1.$$

Return to problem (1). Setting the derivative with respect to zero yields

$$\hat{x}F_1(\hat{x}-1,1) - F = 0 \tag{4}$$

$$F_1 = \frac{F}{\hat{x}} = g > 1$$

A proprietor's income is by comparison

$$k = \underset{x}{\text{Max}} \quad F(x-1,1) - (x-1)$$

$$= F(x-1,1) - (x-1) \quad \text{(say)}$$

$$> F(\hat{x}-1,1) - (\hat{x}-1)$$

$$= 1+\hat{x} \cdot (g-1)$$

or

$$k-1 > \hat{x} \cdot (g-1) \tag{5}$$

The profit margin $k-1$ of a proprietor exceeds the sum of the partners' profit margins.

This implies in particular

$$k > g \tag{6}$$

For otherwise (5) would imply $\hat{x} < 1,$ a contradiction.

We conclude: If a partnership is profitable, a hierarchical organization is even more profitable for the organizer.

A third possibility is that of workers hiring a manager at a salary w between what owners demand and what partners receive as their share in a partnership

$$g < w < k. \tag{7}$$

Now a partner's share will be

$$\operatorname*{Max}_{n} \frac{F(n,1) - w}{n} < \operatorname*{Max}_{x} \frac{F(x-1,1) - g}{x-1}$$

$$= \frac{F(\hat{x}-1,1) - g}{\hat{x}-1} = \frac{F(\hat{x}-1,1)}{\hat{x}} = g$$

This shows that, when workers hire managers, their share falls below that of a pure partnership (cf. Putterman, 1984). We turn next to a comparison of optimal size. The optimum number of partners $\hat{x}$ is determined by (1). The optimal span of control s in a simple proprietorship is found by solving

$$\text{Max}_{s} \quad F(s,1) - s$$

yielding

$$F_1(s,1) - 1 = 0 \tag{8}$$

Comparing (1) and (8) shows that

$$F_1(\hat{x}-1) = \frac{F}{\hat{x}} = g > 1 = F_1(s,1). \tag{9}$$

Since F is assumed to be concave with respect to x_0 $F_1(x_0,x_1)$ is a decreasing function of x_0. Inequality (9) implies therefore that

$$\hat{x}-1 < s. \tag{10}$$

The optimum span of control in a hierarchical organization is larger than that in a partnership (cf. Figure 20.1). A similar argument shows that partnerships with hired managers should also be smaller than proprietorships. This has been found to apply to "worker managed enterprises" as compared to conventional firms by Ward (1958).

In the Cobb-Douglas case

$$g = \text{Max}_{x} \frac{b(x-1)^{\alpha}}{x}$$

is achieved when

$$\alpha b(x-1)^{\alpha-1}x - b(x-1)^{\alpha} = 0$$

$$\hat{x} = \frac{1}{1-\alpha} \tag{11}$$

The conventional $\alpha = \frac{3}{4}$ would thus imply an optimum with four full time partners.

The achieved return g depends on b.

$$g = b \cdot \alpha^{\alpha}(1-\alpha)^{1-\alpha}$$

Compare this to

$$k = b^{\frac{1}{1-\alpha}} \alpha^{\frac{\alpha}{1-\alpha}} (1-\alpha) \tag{12}$$

Evidently

$$k = g^{\frac{1}{1-\alpha}} > g \quad \text{when} \quad g > 1.$$

20.3   Advantage of Partnership: Fixed Shares

Why are partnerships ever chosen if they are less profitable? Presumably because they afford other advantages such as greater freedom; for instance, the freedom to choose one's level of working time or effort.

We discuss this in terms of a specific utility function. Let t be working time, $c-t$ leisure and y income. The utility function to be considered has the simple form (as in Chapter 18)

$$u = h \ln (2-t) + y. \tag{1}$$

We consider two alternatives.

<u>Case 1</u>: Each partner i receives a fixed share of profits a_i regardless of effort t_i. Subsequently we shall specify this to mean equal shares. (The "commune" of Sen, 1966.)

<u>Case 2</u>: Reward y_i is proportional to effort, (the "collective" of Sen, 1966.) Then for partner i

$$y_i = \frac{t_i}{t} \cdot y \quad \text{where} \quad t = \sum_i t_i. \tag{2}$$

In the case of hired employees earning a unit wage for a unit of effort, utility equals

$$u = h \ln (2-t_i) + t_i. \tag{3}$$

When $h = 1$, this is maximized by $t_i = 1$ yielding income $y = 1$ and utility $u = 1$ as bench marks.

If the partnership operates at the optimal level x of combined effort, the marginal product is g. Then

$$y = gt.$$

In the fixed share case, a partner's income equals

$$y_i = g \cdot a_i \cdot (t_i + T) \tag{4}$$

where

$$T = \sum_{j \neq i} t_j \quad \text{is time input by the other partners.}$$

and his/her utility is

$$u_i = h \ln (2-t_i) + g \, a \, (t_i + T). \tag{5}$$

Maximization with respect to t_i yields

$$t_i = 2 - \frac{h}{g}\frac{1}{a_i} \qquad (6)$$

and

$$t = t_i + T = \sum_{i=1}^{n} t_i = 2n - \frac{h}{g}\sum_{i=1}^{n}\frac{1}{a_i} \qquad (7)$$

Notice that a partner's effort t_i is an increasing function of a partner's share a_i. Total effort is maximized when the shares are equal.

When h is too large or a_i too small, the expression in (6) can become negative and must be replaced by zero. Thus

$$t_i = (2 - \frac{h}{g}\frac{1}{a_i})^{+} \qquad (6')$$

A partner with a strong preference for leisure or a small enough share might prefer to do no work at all. This would, of course, not be tolerated in the long run. From now we assume that t_i is strictly positive.

With equal shares one has

$$t_i = 2 - n \cdot \frac{h}{g} \qquad (6'')$$

effort per partner is a strictly decreasing function of the number of partners.

$$t = \sum_i t_i = 2n - n^2\frac{h}{g} \qquad (7')$$

It may appear from this that a partnership with equal shares cannot achieve the optimum combined effort $\hat{x}$ calculated in Section 20.2. For

$$\text{Max } t$$
$$n$$

is obtained when $n = \dfrac{g}{h}$

and equals

$$t = \frac{g}{h} \tag{8}$$

Unless the marginal productivity g of effort remains significantly above the level $\hat{g}$ for an optimal sized partnership ($n = 4$ in the Cobb-Douglas case) as long as n is smaller than $\hat{x}$, then fixed share partnerships will tend to be smaller than is optimal with respect to productivity--they will stay in the range where returns are still increasing, $g > \hat{g}$.

But unless the partners are myopic and do not perceive that g is initially increasing with n, this will not happen as we now show.

In fact, achieved utility per partner is

$$\hat{u} = h \ln \frac{h}{g} \frac{1}{a_i} + a_i g \left(2 - \frac{h}{g} \frac{1}{a_i} \right)$$

$$\hat{u} = h \ln \frac{h}{g} \frac{1}{a_i} + 2 a_i g - h \tag{9}$$

and in the case of equal shares

$$\hat{u} = h \left(\ln n \cdot \frac{h}{g} - 1 \right) + \frac{2g}{n} \tag{9'}$$

Now

$$\frac{d\hat{u}}{dn} = \frac{h}{n} - \frac{2g}{n^2} - \frac{h}{g} \cdot g' + \frac{2g'}{n}$$

$$= \left(\frac{h}{n} - \frac{2g}{n^2} \right) \left(1 - \frac{ng'}{g} \right) \tag{10}$$

The first parenthesis is negative as long as t_i from (6) is positive. The second parenthesis is negative as long as the output elasticity per partner is greater than one, and this is true in the domain of increasing returns.

In the Cobb-Douglas case increasing returns occur when

$$0 \leqslant x \leqslant \frac{1}{1-\alpha}.$$

But $\hat{x} = \frac{1}{1-\alpha}$ is the optimal size of a partnership, cf. (20.2.10).

We return to the question when a partnership with fixed shares is preferred to individual effort. This happens when achieved utility exceeds unity. From (9')

$$\hat{u} = h \ln n \frac{h}{g} + \frac{2g}{n} - h > 1$$

or

$$h(\ln h \cdot \frac{n}{g} - 1) > 1 - \frac{2g}{n}$$

Assume $n = 2$, the smallest type of partnership. Accordingly g will be large since the organization is operating in the regime of increasing returns. Assume $g = 2$. Then

$$t_i = 2-h, \quad t = 4-2h, \quad y = g-4h$$

$$\hat{u} = h \ln h - h + 2 \qquad \text{from (9').}$$

Thus partnership is preferred to individual effort when $\hat{u} > 1$ or

$$h(\ln h-1) > 1 \tag{11}$$

which is true for all $h > 1$.

But can such a partnership ever be preferred to ownership of a simple organization?   Assume

$$g = 3.105 \qquad \text{(as in 17.3)}.$$

Then this partnership is preferred whenever

$$h(\ln h-1) > 3.105 - 2 = 1.105$$

This is not true for any $h < 2$.   But when $h \geq 2$ partner's preferred labor input is zero.   Hence, the required strong preference for leisure would make a fixed share partnership inoperable, even when only two partners are involved.

20.4   Proportional Rewards

Turn next to the case of rewards proportional to input. Utility to the ith partner is

$$u_i = h \ln (2-t_i) + \frac{t_i}{t} \cdot g \cdot t \qquad (1)$$

$$= h \ln (2-t_i) + gt_i .$$

This is maximized by

$$t_i = 2 - \frac{h}{g} \qquad (2)$$

Achieved utility is then

$$\hat{u} = h \ln \frac{h}{g} + 2g - h \qquad (3)$$

Comparison with the fixed equal share case (20.3.9') shows that

$$\hat{u} - \hat{u} = 2g \left(1 - \frac{1}{n}\right) - h \ln n$$

This vanishes for $u = 1$ and increases with n as long as t_i in (6') is positive. Thus

$$\tilde{u} > \hat{u} \tag{4}$$

In any partnership proportional rewards achieves greater utility than fixed shares, a result that should cause no surprise, since the fixed share system discourages effort.

This conclusion is actually true for arbitrary concave utility functions in terms of leisure and income, when shares are equal. Let ϕ denote again the production function.

$$\hat{u} = \underset{t}{\text{Max}} \quad u(c-t, \frac{1}{n} \phi(T+t))$$

Here c is total available time

$$\hat{u} = u(c-\hat{t}, \frac{1}{n} \phi(T+\hat{t})) \qquad (\text{say})$$

$$\hat{u} = u(c-\hat{t}, \frac{1}{n} \phi(n\hat{t}))$$

since $\quad T = (n-1)\hat{t}.$

Rewrite $\quad \hat{u} = u(c-\hat{t}, \frac{\hat{t}}{\hat{t}n} \phi(\hat{t}n))$

$$\hat{u} \leq \underset{t,L}{\text{Max}} \quad u(c-\hat{t}, \frac{t}{L} \phi(L)) = \tilde{u}. \tag{5}$$

Moreover, a partnership with the optimal number of members yields the utility that a benevolent dictator would achieve through central planning for the partnership (ignoring indivisibilities). For central planning would yield exactly the same result as shown by the following

<u>Theorem</u>: When the partnership has the optimal number of members then the distribution proportional to effort achieves the optimum for every member provided the members' preferences are equal.

Proof:

The optimum is given by

$$\text{Max}_{t} \quad u(c-t), \frac{1}{n} \phi(nt))$$

and this is achieved by

$$0 = \frac{\partial u}{\partial t} = -u_1 + u_2 \phi'$$

$$0 = \frac{\partial u}{\partial n} = u_2 \cdot [n\phi' - \phi]/n^2$$

or $\qquad \phi' = \frac{\phi}{nt} \qquad$ average product = marginal product. $\qquad$ (6)

Now consider the utility of an individual member under the proportional distribution.

Let T represent the time input of the other members. The individual is motivated to seek

$$\text{Max}_{t} \quad u(c-t, \frac{t}{T+t} \phi(T+t)).$$

This is achieved by

$$0 = -u_1 + u_2 \cdot [\frac{t\phi' - \phi}{T+t} - \frac{t\phi}{(T+t)^2}].$$

We must show that the bracket equals ϕ'.
Substitution for ϕ' from (6) yields

$$[\quad] = \frac{1}{T+t} (\frac{t}{nt} \phi' + \phi - \frac{t}{T+t} \phi) = \frac{\phi}{T+t} \quad \text{since} \quad nt = T+t$$

$$= \frac{\phi}{T+t} = \frac{\phi}{nt} = \phi' \quad \text{by (6).} \qquad \|$$

When is a partnership with proportional rewards preferred to ownership of a simple organization? Compare the achieved utilities of this partnership $\hat{u}$ from (20.4.3) and the utility of ownership on the simplifying assumption that the owner considers returns to scale to be constant. (This if anything underestimates the advantage of proprietorship.) In Section 18.3 it was shown that then owner's income is proportional to owner's effort

$$y = kx_1 \tag{7}$$

Utility maximization leads to time input

$$x_1 = 2 - \frac{h}{k} \tag{8}$$

and achieved utility

$$u = h \ln \left(\frac{h}{k}\right) + 2k - h \tag{9}$$

Now

$$u - \hat{u} = h \ln \left(\frac{g}{k}\right) + 2 (k-g) < 0$$

if

$$h > \frac{2(k-g)}{\ln \left(\frac{k}{g}\right)} \tag{10}$$

But h is bounded by $t_i \geq 0$ from (2)

$$h \leqslant 2g$$

Substituting this maximial value in (10)

$$g > \frac{k-g}{\ln \frac{k}{g}}$$

or

$$1 + \ln \frac{k}{g} > \frac{k}{g}$$

But this inequality holds only for $\frac{k}{g} < 1$. Thus even partnership with proportional sharing does not offer the same economic attraction (utility) as ownership would.

The conclusion to be derived from this is either that barriers to ownership are stronger than those applying to entering a partnership, or that the utility function should contain other variables besides leisure and money income. As it stands now the economic opportunities of ownership dominate those of a partnership.

Conclusion

No simple conclusion emerges from this analysis. A point
repeatedly made is that what appear to be technical constraints
in an organizational context turn out to be objects of economic
choice, at least in the long run. These include such crucial
variables as size of task, span of control, loss of control, and
the productivity of operatives.

This analysis is incomplete. We have set aside all problems
concerned with flow of personnel through organizations. Some of
these were touched upon in <u>rank and organizations</u>. We plan to
return to these in a separate monograph which will address in a
systematic way these topics

  hiring, firing, and seniority

  promotion probabilities: two levels

  attrition and composition

  promotion systems: multiple levels

  selectivity and quality

  career utility

  monopolistic salary policy

  career choices: effort

  mobility among organizations

Interpersonal differences are an important theme in the
study of flow and promotion processes. But they are relevant
also to the allocation problem considered in this monograph.
Interesting and challenging questions emerge when operatives and
managers are treated not as homogeneous but as heterogeneous with
respect to ability and motivation and also as different in their
preference for risk taking.

The whole area of competition in and among organizations is
beset also by problems of risk taking and of differential access
to capital resources. There remains a great deal to be done in
the economic study of organizations.

Appendix A

<u>Deriving Supervisory Relationships from Control</u>

<u>Lemma</u>: Necessary and sufficient for $\{S_i\}$ to be a collection of control sets is that $j \in S_i$ implies $S_j \subset S_i$.

<u>Proof</u>: Necessity: obvious.
Sufficiency: $S_j \subset S_i \Leftrightarrow i > j$ defines a partial ordering based on set inclusion identical with $i > j$ iff $j \in S_i$.

<u>Problem</u>: From the collection of sets $\{S_i\}$ recover relationship $i = sp\,(j)$.

<u>Lemma</u>: For any $i, k \in \Omega$ either $S_i \cap S_k = \phi$ or $S_i \subset S_k$ or $S_k \subset S_i$.

<u>Lemma</u>: If $j \in S_i$ and $j \in S_k$ then $S_i \subset S_k$ or $S_k \subset S_i$.

<u>Corollary</u>: If $j \in S_i \cap S_k$ then $S_i = S_i \cap S_k$ or $S_k = S_i \cap S_k$.

<u>Theorem</u>: $i = sp\,(j)$ iff $S_i = \bigcap_{k:\ j \in S_k} S_k$.

Appendix B

<u>Average Span of Control and More Graph Theory</u>

The supervisory structure of an organization was discussed in terms of a digraph. For certain purposes the direction of arcs may be ignored so that an ordinary (undirected) graph is obtained.

Notice, first, that this graph of an organization is a tree. The N points of the tree are joined by $N-1$ supervisory links and by $\frac{N(N-1)}{2}$ (undirected) unique paths. There are at least two and at most $N-1$ endpoints, i.e., points of degree one $(N > 2)$. The first bound is reached by a ladder, the second by a star.

$$\text{Let} \quad I = \left\{ i \mid i \neq p, \quad \deg(i) > 1 \right\}$$

be the set of points representing line supervisors. The span of control of any $i \in I$, $i \neq p$ is defined as

$$s_i = \deg(i) - 1 \tag{1}$$

$\deg(i)$ is the <u>degree</u>, the number of lines incident with i. For p the span of control is defined as

$$s_p = \deg(p). \tag{2}$$

Let n_0 be the number of endpoints. Then

$$\bar{s} = \frac{s_p + \sum_{i \in I} s_i}{N - n_0} \tag{3}$$

is the average span of control. We show that $\bar{s}$ depends only on N and n_0.

A well-known formula of graph theory states [Harary, 1971, p. 14]

$$\sum \text{ degrees} = 2 \cdot \text{number of lines} \tag{4}$$

Substituting

$$s_p + \sum_{i \in I} (s_i + 1) + n_o + 2(N-1)$$

$$s_p + \sum_{i \in I} s_i + N - n_o - 1 + n_o = 2(N-1)$$

$$s_p + \sum_{i \in I} s_i = N - 1. \tag{5}$$

Proposition

The sum of all spans of control equals the number of members to be supervised $N-1$.

Furthermore, by (3)

$$\bar{s} = \frac{N-1}{N-n_0}$$

$$= \frac{N-1}{M}. \tag{6}$$

Theorem 1

The average span of control is determined by (6). It is independent of structural detail. In particular, it is independent of the location of p.

Now
$$a_{R+1} = \frac{1+a_R}{\sigma_R}$$

$$\geq \frac{1 + \dfrac{1}{\sigma_{R-1} - 1}}{\sigma_R} = \frac{\sigma_{R-1}}{(\sigma_{R-1} - 1)\sigma_R}$$

$$= \frac{1}{\sigma_R - \dfrac{\sigma_R}{\sigma_{R-1}}}$$

$$\geq \frac{1}{\sigma_R - 1} \quad \text{since} \quad \sigma_R \geq \sigma_{R-1}$$

and since $\sigma_R \geq 2$ because $\sigma_0 \geq 1$. $\|$

Appendix C

<u>Proof of the Lemma for Section 6.9</u>

Proof of $\dfrac{1}{\sigma_R - 1} \leqslant a_{R+1} \leqslant \dfrac{1}{\sigma_R}$ from Section 6.9.

<u>Proof</u>: (induction). When $R = 1$ then

$$a_2 = \frac{1+\sigma_0}{\sigma_0 \sigma_1} \leqslant \frac{1}{\sigma_0} \quad \text{since} \quad \sigma_1 \geqslant 1+\sigma_0$$

Moreover,

$$\frac{1}{\sigma_1 - 1} \leqslant \frac{1+\sigma_0}{\sigma_0 \sigma_1} = a_2$$

since

$$(1+\sigma_0)(\sigma_1 - 1) = \sigma_0 \sigma_1 + \sigma_1 - (\sigma_0 + 1) \geqq \sigma_0 \sigma_1$$

using (6.9.4).

Assume the lemma to be true for $R-1$.

$$\frac{1}{\sigma_{R-1} - 1} \leqq a_R \leqq \frac{1}{\sigma_0}$$

and consider $a_{R+1} = \dfrac{1 + a_R}{\sigma_R}$.

Now $a_{R+1} \leqq \dfrac{1 + \dfrac{1}{\sigma_0}}{\sigma_R} = \dfrac{\sigma_0 + 1}{\sigma_0 \sigma_R} \leqq \dfrac{1}{\sigma_0}$

since $\sigma_R \geqq \sigma_1 \geqq 1+\sigma_0$.

Selected Bibliography

Alchian, A.A. and H. Demsetz, 1972, "Production, Information Costs and Economic Organizations," The American Economic Review, Vol. 62, 777-795.

Antle, Rick and Gary D. Eppen, 1985, "Capital Rationing and Organizational Slack in Capital Budgeting," Management Science, Vol. 31, No. 2, February.

Arrow, Kenneth J., 1974, The Limits of Organization, New York: W.W. Norton.

Bartholomew, David J., 1967, Stochastic Models for Social Processes, John Wiley and Sons, London-New York-Sydney.

Beckenbach, E.F. and R. Bellman, 1961, An Introduction to Inequalities, New York: Random House.

Becker, Selwyn W. and Duncan Neuhauser, 1977, The Efficient Organization, Amsterdam: Elsevier North-Holland.

Beckmann, M.J., 1960, "Returns to Scale in Business Administration," Quarterly Journal of Economics, 74, 464-471.

Beckmann, Martin, 1975, "Echelle des Salaries et Avancement dans les Organisation Hierarchiques," Annales de L'Insee, 18, 45-60.

Beckmann, Martin, 1977a, "Management Production Functions and the Theory of the Firm," Journal of Economic Theory, 14, 1-18.

Beckmann, Martin, 1977b, "On the Ratio of Supervisors to Supervised," Quantitative Wirtschaftsforschung, Festschrift für Wilhelm Krelle (E. Helmstädter and R. Henn, eds.), Tübingen: Mohr, 1977.

Beckmann, Martin J., 1978, Rank in Organizations, New York: Springer-Verlag.

Beckmann, Martin J., 1983, "The Structure of Supervision in Organizations: A Graph Theoretic Approach," in Mathematische Systeme in der Okonomie (Martin J. Beckmann, Wolfgang Eichhorn and Wilhelm Krelle, editors), Maisenheim: Athenaum.

Beckmann, Martin J., 1984, "Hierarchy vs. Partnership," _Journal of Economic Behavior and Organization_, 5, North-Holland, 237-245.

Bell, Gerald D., 1967, "Determinants of the Span of Control," _American Journal of Sociology_, 73, 100-109.

Bendix, R., 1956, _Work and Authority in Industry_, New York: Wiley.

Berge, Claude, 1976, _Graphs and Hypergraphs_, North-Holland.

Blau, Peter M. and W.R. Scott, 1963, _Formal Organization: A Comparative Approach_, London: Routledge and Kegan Paul.

Blau, Peter M., 1973, _Bureaucracy_, London: Institute for Economic Affairs.

Boulding, K.E., 1953, _The Organizational Revolution_, New York: Harper.

The Budget of the United States, 1982, Washington, D.C., U.S. Government Printing Office.

Calvo, C.A., 1979, "Hierarchy, Ability, and Income Distribution," _Journal of Political Economy_, Vol. 87, No. 5.

Caplow, T., 1957, "Organizational Size," _Admin. Sci. Quart._, 1, 484-505.

Chu, David S.C. and John D. White (April, 1975), "Developing the Military Executive," _Commission on the Organization of the Personnel for the Conduct of Foreign Policy_, Vol. 6, Appendices, 250-272.

Clark, James W. (April, 1975), Foreign Affairs Personnel Management, _ibid._, 181-222.

Coase, R.H., 1937, "The Nature of the Firm," _Economica_, Vol. 4, 386-405.

Collins, P., 1962, "Career Contingencies of English University Teachers," _British Journal of Sociology_, 13, 286-293.

Cooper, W.W., et al., 1962, _New Perspectives in Organization Research_, New York: Wiley.

Cox, D.R., 1967, _Renewal Theory_, London: Methuen.

Cyert, R.M. and J.G. March, 1963, A Behavioral Theory of the
     Firm, Englewood Cliffs, New Jersey: Prentice-Hall.

Downs, A., 1967, Inside Bureaucracy, Boston: Little, Brown.

Dressler, Gary, 1980, Organization Theory, Englewood Cliffs:
     Prentice-Hall.

Drucker, Peter, 1954, The Practice of Management, New York:
     Harper.

Entwisle, Doris R. and J. Walton, 1961, "Observations on the Span
     of Control, Admin. Sci. Quarterly, 5, 522-533.

Fama, Eugene, 1980, "Agency Problems and the Theory of the Firm,"
     Journal of Political Economy, 88, 288-307.

Gannon, M.J., 1977, Management: An Organizational Perspective,
     Boston: Little, Brown.

Goode, William J., 1978, The Celebration of Heroes: Prestige and
     the Social Control System. Berkeley: University of
     California Press.

Grossman, Sanford and Oliver Hart, 1983, "An Analysis of the
     Principal-Agent Problem," Econometrica, 51, 7-45.

Groves, Theodore, 1973, "Incentives in Teams," Econometrica, Vol.
     41, 617-631.

Groves, T., 1976, "Incentive Compatible Control of Decentralized
     Organizations," in Y. Ho and S. Mitters (eds.), Directions
     in Large Scale Systems: Many-Person Optimization and
     Decentralized Control, New York, Plenum.

Harary, Frank, 1971, Graph Theory, Addison-Wesley Publishing
     Company, Reading, Massachusetts.

Harris, M., C.H. Kriebel and A. Raviv, 1982, "Asymmetric
     Information, Incentives and Intrafirm Resource Allocation,"
     Management Science, 28 (6), 604-620.

Hayek, Friedrich A., 1945, "The Use of Knowledge in Society,"
     American Economic Review, 35, 519-530.

Hax, Arnoldo G. and Nicolas S. Majluf, 1981, "Organizational Design: A Survey and an Approach," Operations Research, 29 (3), 417-446.

Healey, J.H., 1956, "Coordination and Control of Executive Functions," Personnel, 33, 106-117.

Henn, R. and H.P. Künzi, 1968, Einführung in die Unternehmensforschung, I, II, Springer-Verlag, Berlin-Heidelberg-New York.

Hess, James D., 1983, The Economics of Organization, Amsterdam: North-Holland.

Holmstrom, Bengt, 1977, On Incentives and Control in Organizations, Ph.D. dissertation, Stanford University.

Holmstrom, Bengt, 1979, "Moral Hazard and Observability," Bell Journal of Economics, 10, 74-91.

Holmstrom, Bengt, 1982, "Moral Hazard in Teams," Bell Journal of Economics, Vol. 13, No. 2, 324-340.

Indik, B.P., 1963, "Some Effects of Organization Size on Member Attitudes and Behavior," Hum. Relat., 16, 369-384.

Knight, F., 1921, 1964, Risk, Uncertainty and Profit. New York: A.M. Kelley.

Koontz, Harold and Cyril P. O'Donnell, 1959, Principles of Management, New York: McGraw-Hill.

Koopmans, T.C., 1969, "Note on a Social System Composed of Hierarchies with Overlapping Personnel," Orbis Economicus, July.

Langer, Elinor, 1970, "Inside the New York Telephone Company," Women at Work, Quadrangle/The New York Times Book Co., 307-360.

Lundberg, Shelly J. and Richard Startz, 1983, "Private Discrimination and Social Intervention in Competitive Labor Markets," American Economic Review, Vol. 73, 340-347.

Lydall, H., 1968, The Structure of Earnings, Oxford: Clarendon Press.

Mackenzie, R.D., 1974, "Measuring a Person's Capacity for Interaction," Organizational Behavior, October, 149-169.

March, James G. and Herbert A. Simon, 1958, Organization, New
  York: Wiley.
March, James G., 1965, Handbook of Organization, Chicago: Rand-
  McNally.
Marglin, Stephen, 1974, "What Do Bosses Do? The Origins and
  Functions of Hierarchy in Capitalist Production," The Review
  of Radical Political Economy, 6, 33-60.
Marschak, Jacob, 1952, "Teams and Organizations under
  Uncertainty," Cowles Commission Discussion Paper 2034.
Marschak, J., 1956, "Remarks on the Rationale of Leadership,"
  Cowles Foundation Discussion Paper #6.
Marschak, J. and R. Radner, 1972, Economic Theory of Teams, New
  Haven: Yale University Press.
Marschak, J., 1977, "Efficient Organizational Design," Western
  Management Science Institute, Working Paper #273.
Marshall, A., 1891, Principles of Economics, London: Macmillan.
McGregor, D., 1960, The Human Side of Enterprise, New York:
  McGraw-Hill.
McGuire, C.B. and Roy Radner, 1972, 1986 second edition, Decision
  and Organization, Amsterdam: North-Holland.
McNulty, J.E., 1956-1957, "Administrative Costs and Scale of
  Operations in the U.S. Electrical Power Industry--A
  Statistical Study," Journal of Industrial Economics, 5, 30-
  43.
Merton, R.K., 1957, Social Theory and Social Structure (rev.
  ed.), Glencoe, Illinois: Free Press.
Milgrom, Paul, 1981, "Good News and Bad News: Representation
  Theorems and Applications," Bell Journal of Economics, 380-
  391.
Mirrlees, James, 1976, "The Optimal Structure of Incentives and
  Authority Within an Organization," Bell Journal of
  Economics, Vol. 7, No. 1.
Miyazaki, H., 1977, "The Rat Race and Internal Labour Markets,"
  Bell Journal of Economics, Vol. 8, No. 2.

Mouzelis, N.P., 1968, Organization and Bureaucracy: An Analysis
    of Modern Theories, Chicago, Illinois: Aldine Publishing.

Osborn, R.C., 1951, "Efficiency and Profitability in Relation to
    Size," Harvard Business Review, 29 (2), 82-94.

Penrose, E.T., 1959, The Theory of the Growth of the Firm, New
    York: Wiley.

Phelps, Edmund S., 1972, "The Statistical Theory of Racism and
    Sexism," American Economic Review, Vol. 62, 659-661.

Price, Derek J. de Solla, 1963, Little Science, Big Science, New
    York: Columbia University Press.

Putterman, Louis, 1984, "On Some Recent Explanations of Why
    Capital Hires Labor," Economic Inquiry, Vol. 22, 171-87.

Putterman, Louis, 1986, The Economic Nature of the Firm. A
    Reader, Cambridge: Cambridge University Press.

Radner, Roy, 1981, "Monitoring Cooperative Agreements in a
    Repeated Principal-Agent Relationship," Econometrica, 49,
    1127-1148.

Radner, Roy, 1985, "Decentralization and Incentives," New
    Jersey: AT&T Bell Laboratories.

Radner, Roy, 1985, "The Internal Economy of Large Firms," Murray
    Hill, New Jersey: AT&T Bell Laboratories.

Roberts, D.R., 1956, "A General Theory of Executive Compensation
    Based on Statistically Tested Propositions," Quarterly
    Journal of Economics, 20, 270-294.

Roberts, D.R., 1959, Executive Compensation, Glencoe, Illinois:
    The Free Press.

Rosen, Sherwin, 1981, "Output, Income and Rank in Hierarchical
    Firms," Chicago: Economics Research Center NORC Discussion
    Paper #81-10.

Rosen, Sherwin, 1982, "Authority, Control and the Distribution of
    Earnings," Bell Journal of Economics, Vol. 13, No. 2, 311-
    323.

Rosen, Sherwin, 1986, "Prizes and Incentives in Elimination
    Tournaments," American Economic Review, 76 (4), 701-715.

Rosenblatt, D., 1956, "Foundations of a Stochastic Theory of
    Organization," (Abstract), Econometrica, 24, 2 (April), 205-
    6.

Ross, N.S., 1952-1953, "Management and the Size of the Firm,"
    Review of Economic Studies, 19 (3), 148-154.

Ross, Stephen, 1973, "The Economic Theory of Agency: The
    Principal's Problem," American Economic Review, 63, 134-139.

Sah, Raaj Kumar and Joseph E. Stiglitz, 1986, "The Architecture
    of Economic Systems: Hierarchies and Polyarchies," American
    Economic Review, 76 (4), 716-727.

Sato, R.S., 1981, Theory of Technical Change and Economic
    Invariance: Application of Lie Groups, Academic Press.

Seal, H.L., 1945, "The Mathematics of a Population Composed of
    Stationary Strata each Recruited from the Stratum Below and
    Supported at the Lowest Level by a Uniform Annual Number of
    Entrants," Biometrika, 33, 226-230.

Sen, Amartya K., 1966, "Labor Allocation in a Cooperative Enter-
    prise," Review of Economic Studies, 33, 361-71.

Sen, A., 1970, Collective Choice and Social Welfare, San
    Francisco: Holden Day.

Shavell, Steven, 1979, "Risk Sharing and Incentives in the
    Principal and Agent Relationship," Bell Journal of
    Economics, 10, 55-73.

Simon, H., et al., 1941, "Workloads of Professional Staff in a
    Public Welfare Agency," Chicago, Am. Publ. Welf. Assoc.

Simon, H., 1951, "A Formal Theory of the Employment Relation,"
    Econometrica.

Simon, Herbert A., 1965, Administrative Behavior; a Study of
    Decision-Making Processes in Administrative Organization,
    2nd edition, New York: Free Press, 26-28.

Simon, Herbert, 1957, "The Compensation of Executives,"
    Sociometry, 20, 32-35.

Simon, Herbert, 1976, _Administrative Behavior_, New York: The
    MacMillan Company, 3rd edition.

Simon, H., 1982, _Models of Bounded Rationality_, Cambridge: MIT
    Press, 14-24.

Simpson, R.L., 1959, "Vertical and Horizontal Communication in
    Formal Organizations," _Admin. Sci. Quarterly_, 4, 188-196.

Smith, Adam, 1776, 1937, _The Wealth of Nations_ (Edwin Cannon,
    ed.). New York: Modern Library.

Spence, A. Michael, 1973, "Job Market Signalling," _Quarterly
    Journal of Economics_, Vol. 87, 355-374.

Spence, A.M., 1975, "The Economics of Internal Organization: An
    Introduction," _The Bell Journal of Economics_, Vol. 6,
    Spring.

Starbuck, William H., 1964, _Mathematics and Organization Theory_,
    Lafayette: Purdue University.

Starbuck, W.H., 1964, "Organizational Growth and Development," in
    J.G. March (ed.), _Handbook of Organizations_, Chicago: Rand-
    McNally & Co.

Stigler, George, 1946, _The Theory of Price_. New York:
    Macmillan.

Stiglitz, Joseph, 1974, "Incentives and Risk-Sharing in Share-
    cropping," _Review of Economic Studies_, 61, 219-256.

Stiglitz, J., 1975, "Incentives, Risk, and Information: Notes
    Toward a Theory of Hierarchy," _The Bell Journal of
    Economics_, Vol. 6, No. 2.

Stoner, J.A.F., 1978, _Management_, Englewood Cliffs, New Jersey:
    Prentice-Hall.

Suojanen, W.W., 1955, "The Span of Control--Fact or Fable?"
    Advanced Management, 20 (11), 5-13.

Taylor, Frederick W., 1911, 1947, _The Principles of Scientific
    Management_. New York: Norton & Co.

Terrien, F.W. and D.L. Mills, 1955, "The Effect of Changing Size
    Upon the Internal Structure of Organizations," _American
    Sociological Review_, 20, 11-13.

Thorellis, H.B., 1965, "Salary Span of Control," _Journal of Monetary Studies_, 2, 269-302.

Tinbergen, Jan, 1964, _Central Planning_, New Haven: Yale University Press.

Tuck, R.A., _An Essay on Rank_, Basil Blackwell.

U.S. Civil Service Commission, 1976, _Executive Personnel in the Federal Service_, Washington: Superintendent of Documents, Stock No. 006-000-00979-4.

Urwick, L.F., 1956, "The Manager's Span of Control," _Harvard Business Review_, 34 (3), 39-47.

Vajda, S., 1947, "The Stratified Semi-Stationary Population," _Biometrika_, 34, 243-254.

Wagner, Harvey M., 1969, _Principles of Operations Research_, Englewood Cliffs: Prentice-Hall.

Ward, Benjamin, 1958, "The Firm in Illyria: Market Syndicalism," _American Economic Review_, 48, 566-89.

Weber, Max, 1925, Wirtschaft und Gesellschaft, Grundriss der Sozialoekonomik, III, Abteilung, 2. Auflage, 1. Halbband, Tübingen: J.C.B. Mohr.

Welch, Finis, 1981, "Affirmative Action and Its Enforcement," _American Economic Review_, Papers and Proceedings, Vol. 71, 127-133.

Williamson, Oliver E., 1967, "Hierarchies Control and Optimum Firm Size," _Journal of Political Economy_, University of Chicago Press, 123-138.

Williamson, O.E., 1970, _Corporate Control and Business Behavior_, New Jersey: Prentice-Hall.

Williamson, Oliver E., 1975, _Markets and Hierarchies_, New York: The Free Press.

Williamson, O., 1985, _The Economic Institutions of Capitalism_, New York: The Free Press.

Name Index

A
Ancot, J.P., ix

B
Beckenbach, E. 58, 137
Beckmann, M.J., 11, 132, 155, 167
Beije, P., ix
Bellman, R., 58, 137

C
Cox, B.R. 116
Cayley, R.W.,40

D
Daganzos, C., x

F
Fischer, J., x
Frommelt, H., x

H
Harary, F., 38, 40
Haverstein, H., ix

K
Knight, F., 2, 209
Kuiper, H., ix

L
Lydall, H., 164

M
Mittermeier, H., x

P
Putterman, L., 214
Paelinck, J., ix

R
Rosenblatt, D., x

S
Schäffler, S., x
Schuler, W., x
Sen, A., 216
Smith, A., 53
Starbuck, W., 57
Stigler, G., 2
Ströhlein, I., x

T
Ten Raa, T., ix
Tinbergen, J., ii

W
Wagner, H., 117
Wathey, M., iv
Weber, M., 54
Williamson, O., 145

Subject Index

A

Ability, 90, 226
Accountability, 8
Acyclic, 10, 31
Acyclicity, 13, 17
Advantage of partnership, 216-221
Agents, 189-192
Allocation in Organization, iv
   of inputs, 159-162
Alternatives to hierarchy, 211-225
Arithmetic mean, 58
Army, 54
Art, 170, 201
Assignment, 71-85, 97
   full-time, 51-55
   part-time, 53
   principle, 25, 26
   rank-minimizing, 80, 81
Asymmetric, 10,16
Auditing, 109
Author, 122
Authority, 3
Average cost, 92, 101
   distance, 35, 36
   rank, 87-88, minimum, 159
   wage, v, 92-94, 101, 102, 105, 106

B

Board, 6
Branch, 15, 17, 39
Budget, 66, 116, 159
Budgeting, vi, 134-139
Bureaucracy, 54
Business firm, 54

C

California, 116
Capacity, 86, 120, 144, 154, 173
   constraints, 96
Capital, 201, 226
Career, 15
Case, 109, 111
   flow, 120
   load, 109, 116
   work, 121
Caseworker, 109, 111, 115
Center, 35, 38, 39, 42
Central planning, 210, 222
Chain of command, 12, 14, 25, 26, 34, 35,
         41, 42, 50, 97

critical, 26, 27
  of control, 18
Chairman, assistant, 15
Channel, 12, 144
Checking, 121, 128-129
Church, 54
Clients, 6
Cobb-Douglas production function, 115 134, 135,
          147, 153, 158, 159, 161, 163, 164, 165,
          167, 169, 175, 179, 187, 192, 198, 206,
          207, 208, 209, 215, 219, 220
Coefficient, technical, 153
Collective, 217
Command and control, 3
  unified, 10
Commune, 211, 216
Communication, 12, 15
  channels of, 33, 143
  path, 34
  network, 33, 37
Comparability, 25
Compensation, 29, 182, 189, 217
Competition, perfect, 160
Completion rate, 110
Congress, Library of, 76
Connectivity, 13
Constraints, 7
Control, 16f, 121, 227
  loss of, vi, 108, 145-147, 201-204, 226
  loss factor, 203
  loss, optimal, 147
  set, 17-20, 29, 227
Coordination, 1,3
Cost, 88, 90-106
  and scale, 101-107
  function, 161, 162; long run 167-169;
          medium run, 165-166
  minimization, 94-96, 151-153, 159
  minimizing, efficient, 96
Counting, up, v, 26, 28, 38, 42, 74
  down, v, 25, 38, 42, 143
  relationships, 24-28
Cycle, 13

        D
Degree, 39, 41, 42, 228, 229
Department lines, v, 77-78
Detection probability, 128
Diameter, 35, 89
Digraph, 11f, 33, 228
Directing, 126
Distance, 25, 33-39, 50
  aggregate, 38, 39
  average, 88-89; from president, 89
  from president, 59

maximal, 37, 38
Distribution, exponential, 110, 116
  uniform, 130-131, 138
Divisibility, 56, 74
Divison, 173
  of labor, 3, 8, 53
  of task, 42

          E
Earnings, individual's, 207
Eccentricity, 35, 37, 38
Economic choice, 49, 226
Economy, 4
  of scale, 171
Efficiency, vi, 3, 44, 159
  criterion, 94
  price, 96
  unit, 43, 180
Effort, 171, 182, 216, 217, 218, 222
Elasticity, 120, 162, 166
  constant, 91
  short run, 166
Employment, full-time, 54
  part-time, 45, 51
Entrepreneur, 206, 209
Entrepreneurship, 201, 214
Enumeration, 40
Equal sharing, 212-216
Equivalence class, 21, 22
Erasmus Universiteit, iii
Error, 128
Estimate, unbiased, 139
Estimation, 63-71

          F
Fellow researcher, 123
First line supervisors, 83
Fixed share, 216-221
Function, concave, 114, 127, 132, 175, 215, 222
  convex, 127, 132, 161
  Lagrange, 136, 163
  production, vi, 5, 111, 112, 118,
          119, 126-127, 160, 173, 181,
          182, 183, 196, 212, 222, see also
          Cobb-Douglas
Functions of organizations, vi, 2
Funds, 134, 135, 137

          G
Geometric mean, 58
  series, 103
German Army, 67
Government, 54

Graph, 33, 228
  directed, see digraph 11f
  theory, 228-229

          H
Height, 35, 61, 84, 86, 88, 97, 101,
          102, 103, 106, 107, 159, 166,
          169
  minimum, 50
  optimal, 166-167
Hierarchical organization, 9, 215
Hierarchy, vi, 57, 87, 210, 211
  alternatives to, vi
  economics of, 196-210
Homogeneous, 153
Hospital, 54

          I
Income, 189, 216, 217, 225
  of owner, 190, 194, 213
Increase, exponential, 87
Individual, 3, 170-173, 207, 209, 210
  independent, 188, 210
  work, 184
Industry, 209-210
Inequality, vi, 3, 18, 210
Information, cost 122-129
  cost of, 108
Information filtering, 143
  full, 134-139
  generating, 144-145
  imperfect, 130
  incomplete, 139-142
  loss of, vi, 108, 130-142, 143-147
  loss rate, 143
  processing, 143
Input, 151, 155, 156, 160
Inspection, 116
Insurance claim, 109
Integer, 52, 56, 73, 79, 98, 148, 150, 151
  assignment, 72-73
Interaction, 123, 124
Irreflexive, 10, 16

          J
Jensen's inequality, 137
Job allocation, v, 96-98

          L
Labor cost, 92, 95
  market, 29, 151
  productivity, 145, 148-149, 150, 171,

203, 226
  requirement, 149
  unions, 54
Ladder, 17, 18, 22, 30, 39, 228
Lagrange function, 136, 163
Law suits, 109
Leanness, V, 78-81
Leisure, 30, 183, 189, 216, 225
  preference for, 185, 190, 195, 218, 221,
      222
Liberty, 210
Line, 229
Linear program, feasible, 96
Long run, 166-169, 205, 226

      M
Management, 47, 54, 129, 147, 155-159
  and Budget, Office of, 66, 75
  by committee, 31
  by delegation, vi, 157, 192, 196-198, 200
  by team-work, 157, 196
  functions, 172
  is management, 157
  motivation, 182-195
  perfect, 4, 41-108, 130
  production function, 156, 169
  size, 77
Manager, hired, 214, 215
Manager's compensation, 193, 195, 201, 202
  productivity, 137
  surplus, 133
Managers, 55, 94, 135, 181, 182
  allocation of, 56-57
  for operatives, v
  to operatives, ratio of, 61
Managerial capacity, 42
  effort, 201
  functions, 142
  labor, 155, 173, 186, 188, 189, 190, 193
  talent, 201
  work, 48, 49, 50, 51, 174, 180
Marginal product, 113, 120, 123, 223
  productivity, 189, 219
Market, 3, 7
  competitive, 7, 210
  economy, 7
Maximal element, 19
Medium run, 163-166
Merit, 90
Message, 33
Money income, 29
Monitor, 183-186
Monopolist, 210
Monotone, 61, 161
Motivation, 4, 226

of organization, 170

        N
National Science Foundation, iv
Norm, 34

        O
Office, 29, 156
  attributes of, 30
Operative, 4, 26, 55, 63, 136, 143, 155
  full-time, 72
  labor, 107, 145, 171, 173, 188
  number of, 46
Opportunity cost, 92, 96
  wage, 171, 172, 177, 178, 181, 200,
        201, 211
Order, partial, 17-19
  complete, 22
  simple, 21, 22-24
Organization, 1, 170-225
  advantage of, 92, 170, 196, 200, 210;
        advantage of simple, 177-180
  balanced, 27, 32, 35, 36, 42, 50, 51,
        59, 63, 67, 84, 86, 89
  efficient, 99
  hierarchical, 9, 192, 209
  large, 46, 90, 93
  multi-level, 143-147, 155-169, 200
  nonbalanced, 68
  nonregular, 104-107
  parts of, 12
  profit-making, 182
  properietary, 5, 211
  quasi-regular, 35, 39
  regular, 85-89, 98, 99, 100, 101, 102, 103
  simple, 72, 97, 107, 109, 130-142,
        148-154, 171, 173-180, 182,
        196, 200, 205, 207, 209, 210, 211
  size of, 43, 45, 47, 52, 83, 84, 100, 107
Organizations, unbalanced, 84
Organizational chart, 11f, 14f, 32, 33, 37,
        40, 41, 49, 63, 72, 78, 84
  design, vi, 45, 47, 48, 78, 96
  efficient, 79, 96
  multiplier, 46, 94
Organization's task, v
Output, 47, 57-58, 111, 148
Output elasticity, 135, 152, 153, 158, 176, 220
  expected, 130, 139
  largest, 58
  optimum, 167
  per supervisor, 121
  price, 205
  quality of 113

Overload, 143
Owner, 182
Ownership, 221, 224

          P
Partial ordering, 227;
  strict, 18
Participating, 126
Partner's income, 212
  share, 214
Partnership, 5, 211, 215, 222
  optimal sized, 219, 220
Party, 54
Path, shortest, 34
Penalty, 183, 185
Perquisites, 21, 29, 211
Person unit, 43, 44
Personnel, 6
  flow of, 226
  minimal, 95
Physics, 122
Pollacek-Kintchin formula, 117
Positions, 10
  full-time, 94
  of rank, 63, 64-67, 104
  supervisory, 12
Power, 29
  scale, 91
Precedence, 21, 30f
  order, 18
Predecessor, 12, 19
President, 9, 17, 42, 64, 78, 83, 97, 143,
          155, 157, 192, 200, 201, 202, 204,
          210
President's capacity, 51, 71
  time, 49
Presidential compensation, 204, 205
Prestige, 29
  of organization, 30
  of rank, 30f
  professional, 30
Principal, 183-186, 195
  and agent, 182-195
Probability distribution, 130
Productivity coefficient, 176
Product, final, 155
Production function, vi, 5, 111, 112, 118,
          119, 126-127, 160, 173, 181, 182,
          183, 196, 212, 222
  bounded, 114, 115, 145
  coefficient, 205
  concave, 152
  for team work, 204
  homogeneous, 113, 172, 206
  linear homogeneous, 129, 132, 148, 151,

154, 156, 169, 186-189, 192, 195
  197, 199
  managerial, 201
  nested, 157, 159, 199, 202
  organizational, 157-168, 169, 171,
    202, 204
Production functions, uses of, 148-154
Productivity, 107-169, 181
  coefficient, 206
  per time, 125
Professions, 170, 171
Profit, 2, 178, 180, 185, 186, 194, 195,
    200, 211, 216
  margin, 214
  share, 182, 189, 190, 191, 211, 218
Profitability, 190
Proportional rewards, 221

      Q
Qualification, 171, 180-181
Queuing, 109-112

      R
Radius, 36
Random, arrival, 109
  search, 128
Rank, v, 4, 8ff, 15, 21ff, 24, 57, 90,
    92, 211
  assignment, v, 25-28, 32
  cardinal, 28
  highest, 21
  in Organization, iii
  minimal, 73
  minimizing, 92
  number, 21, 24
  ordinal, 28
  zero, 26, 27, 28, 71, 73, 86, 88, 97
Ranking member, 19, 30
Reflexive, 22
Research, 121, 122
  team, 122-129
  time, 124
Return, 134, 216
  diminishing, 158
  increasing, 209, 219, 220
  to organization, 177, 178
Returns to scale, 176, 181, 195, 202, 224
  constant, 62, 154, 173, 178, 203, 204, 206
  diminishing, 141, 180
  increasing, 62, 153, 154, 192-195, 206, 211,
    212, 213
  in management, vi
  of management, 107
Returns to substitution, 127

diminishing, 174
Risk, 171, 212
  aversion, 178, 226
Rotation, 211

        S
Salary, 21, 29, 214
  factor, 165
  increase, 92
  of rank, 160
  range, 90
  scale, 167
  schedule, 90-92, exponential, 91, 101,
        linear, 91, power scale, (91)
  span, 153
  structure, 102
Scale, 4
Search effort, 128
Semi-path, 13
Seniority, 31, 90
Set inclusion, 18, 227
Share, equal, 219, 221
Shirking, 183
Short run, 55, 56-57, 96, 160-162
Size, v, 145, 211, 218
  optimal, vi, 212, 222
Slack, 72, 86, 159
S-ladder, 73, 104, 105
Social science, 122
Source, 13
Sources, of support, 6
Span of control, 15, 39, 41-43, 53, 55, 56,
        63, 102, 106, 121, 130, 139, 145,
        149, 179, 180, 182, 184, 185, 202,
        203, 226, 228
  and rank, 59-63
  average, 57-58, 63, 65, 67, 70, 83,
        228-229,
  constant, 36, 44-48, 86
  maximal, 42, 86
  optimal, 122, 133, 141, 153, 163-165,
        176, 215
  uniform, v, 44, 56, 58, 65, 86, 146, 159
  presidential, 36
Spezialization, 171
Staff, 14, 106
  increasing line, 106
Standard deviation, 131
Star, 39, 228
Subordinate, 14
Subsistance, 191
Substitutability, 108
Substitution, v, 109-121, 150
Subtask, 4, 126
Succession, 30

Supervising, manager, 41
  operatives, 41, 83
  supervisors, 83
Supervision, 4, 8-16, 41, 57, 149, 150-151,
       155, 156, 157, 171, 182, 196,
      227, 228
  amount of = supervision, number of, 45
  content of, 9f
  cost of, v
  delegated, 211
  effective, 184
  full-time, 53
  multiple, 15
  of operatives, 57
  structure of, 10f
Supervisor, 14, 57, 63, 64, 109, 111, 116,
       130, 144, 164, 228
  assignment of, 32
  first-line, 57, (62)
  full-time, 54, 65, 72
Supervisors', allocation on, v
Supervisors, number of, 46, 159
Supervisory, load, 55, 57,
  relationship, number of, 47
Supply function, 190
Support, 81-84
  personnel, 29, 54, 81
Surplus, 211
Symmetric, 22

      T
Targets, vi, 130-134
Task, 4, 8, 48, 86
  size, 43, 44, 71, 98, 149, 167, 226
Tax, 29
  returns, 109
Team, management, vi
  leader, 124
  member, 123, 124, access to, 124
  optimal size of, vi, 123
  work, 121, 204-205
Territorial division, 42
Title, 21, 29
Top management, vi
Transitive, 16, 22
Tree, 11, 35, 228
  labelled, 40
  unlabelled rooted, 40

      U
Unit, cost, 89, (101), 152,
      159, 169, 204, minimal, 154,
      minimum of, 167
  labor cost, v, 92-94, 98-101, 105, 106

of output, 60, 172
  wage, 205
Utility, 2, 29, 90, 195, 217, 223, 225
  achieved, 220, 221, 222, 224
  function, 90–91, 192, 193, 216
  linear, 91
  logarithmic, 91, 189
  maximizing, 189

V

Variable, dual, 96
  standardized, 118
Variance, 117, 130, 140
Von Thünen's wage formula, 191

W

Wage, 203
  rate, 180, 205
  ratio, 153, 164
  structure, vi, 200–201, 204
Weber point, 39
Welfare, agency, 109–121
  applicants, 109
Work, full-time, 191, 195, 212–216
  operative, 44, 45, 52, 54, 71, 84, 94,
      129, 174, 180
  part-time, 180, 210
  supervisory, 45, 59, 60,
Worker, 111
Writing, 170, 201